ULTIMATE
Singer - Songwriter
GUITAR COLLECTION

Project Manager: Aaron Stang
Art Layout/Design: Ken Rehm

ARTIST INDEX

AMERICA A HORSE WITH NO NAME 85 • TIN MAN 169

JACKSON BROWNE THE ROAD 130 • ROSIE 140

JIMMY BUFFETT COME MONDAY 52 • A PIRATE LOOKS AT 40 123

HARRY CHAPIN CATS IN THE CRADLE 18 • TAXI 158

BRUCE COCKBURN WONDERING WHERE THE LIONS ARE 177

SHERYL CROW ALL I WANNA DO 4 • STRONG ENOUGH 151

JOHN DENVER MY SWEET LADY 120 • SUNSHINE ON MY SHOULDERS 166
TAKE ME HOME COUNTRY ROADS 154

EAGLES LYIN' EYES 106 • TAKE IT EASY 136

STEVE EARLE FEARLESS HEART 60 • GOOD OL' BOY (GETTIN' TOUGH) 63

JANIS IAN DAYS LIKE THESE 50 • SOCIETY'S CHILD 148

JEWEL WHO WILL SAVE YOUR SOUL 182 • YOU WERE MEANT FOR ME 186

GORDON LIGHTFOOT EARLY MORNING RAIN 55 • IF YOU COULD READ MY MIND 100

LOGGINS & MESSINA HOUSE AT POOH CORNER 90

THE MAMAS AND THE PAPAS CALIFORNIA DREAMIN' 24 • CREEQUE ALLEY 48

DON McLEAN AND I LOVE YOU SO 10 • VINCENT (STARRY, STARRY NIGHT) 172

JONI MITCHELL BOTH SIDES NOW 26 • CHELSEA MORNING 36 • THE CIRCLE GAME 31

ALANIS MORISSETTE UNINVITED 180 • YOU LEARN 190

VAN MORRISON AND IT STONED ME 15 • CRAZY LOVE 44

NITTY GRITTY DIRT BAND MR. BOJANGLES 111

CAT STEVENS THE FIRST CUT IS THE DEEPEST 68 • I LOVE MY DOG 97

JAMES TAYLOR COPPERLINE 40 • MILLWORKER 114 • SHOWER THE PEOPLE 143

NEIL YOUNG HARVEST MOON 70 • HEART OF GOLD 76
ONLY LOVE CAN BREAK YOUR HEART 128

CONTENTS

ALL I WANNA DO SHERYL CROW 4

AND I LOVE YOU SO DON McLEAN 10

AND IT STONED ME VAN MORRISON 15

BOTH SIDES NOW JONI MITCHELL 26

CALIFORNIA DREAMIN' THE MAMAS AND THE PAPAS 24

CATS IN THE CRADLE HARRY CHAPIN 18

CHELSEA MORNING JONI MITCHELL 36

THE CIRCLE GAME JONI MITCHELL 31

COME MONDAY JIMMY BUFFETT 52

COPPERLINE JAMES TAYLOR 40

CRAZY LOVE VAN MORRISON 44

CREEQUE ALLEY THE MAMAS AND THE PAPAS 48

DAYS LIKE THESE JANIS IAN 50

EARLY MORNING RAIN GORDON LIGHTFOOT 55

FEARLESS HEART STEVE EARLE 60

THE FIRST CUT IS THE DEEPEST CAT STEVENS 68

GOOD OL' BOY (GETTIN' TOUGH) STEVE EARLE 63

HARVEST MOON NEIL YOUNG 70

HEART OF GOLD NEIL YOUNG 76

A HORSE WITH NO NAME AMERICA 85

HOUSE AT POOH CORNER LOGGINS & MESSINA 90

I LOVE MY DOG CAT STEVENS 97

IF YOU COULD READ MY MIND GORDON LIGHTFOOT 100

LYIN' EYES EAGLES 106

MILLWORKER JAMES TAYLOR 114

MR. BOJANGLES NITTY GRITTY DIRT BAND 111

MY SWEET LADY JOHN DENVER 120

ONLY LOVE CAN BREAK YOUR HEART NEIL YOUNG 128

A PIRATE LOOKS AT 40 JIMMY BUFFETT 123

THE ROAD JACKSON BROWNE 130

ROSIE JACKSON BROWNE 140

SHOWER THE PEOPLE JAMES TAYLOR 143

SOCIETY'S CHILD JANIS IAN 148

STRONG ENOUGH SHERYL CROW 151

SUNSHINE ON MY SHOULDERS JOHN DENVER 166

TAKE IT EASY EAGLES 136

TAKE ME HOME COUNTRY ROADS JOHN DENVER 154

TAXI HARRY CHAPIN 158

TIN MAN AMERICA 169

UNINVITED ALANIS MORISSETTE 180

VINCENT (STARRY, STARRY NIGHT) DON McLEAN 172

WHO WILL SAVE YOUR SOUL JEWEL 182

WONDERING WHERE THE LIONS ARE BRUCE COCKBURN 177

YOU LEARN ALANIS MORISSETTE 190

YOU WERE MEANT FOR ME JEWEL 186

ALL I WANNA DO

Words and Music by
SHERYL CROW, WYN COOPER, KEVIN GILBERT,
BILL BOTTRELL and DAVID BAERWALD

All I Wanna Do - 6 - 1

*Gtr. III is tuned to open E ⑥ = E ⑤ = B ④ = E ③ = G♯ ② = B ① = E

All I Wanna Do - 6 - 4

Verse 2:
I like a good beer buzz early in the morning,
And Billy likes to peel the labels, from his bottles of Bud.
And shred them on the bar.
Then he lights every match in an oversized pack.
Letting each one burn down to his thick fingers.
Before blowing and cursing them out.
And he's watching the Buds as they spin on the floor.
A happy couple enters the bar dancing dangerously close to one another.
The bartender looks up from his want ads.
(To Chorus:)

AND I LOVE YOU SO

Words and Music by
DON McCLEAN

Gtr. 1: Capo III

Intro
Moderately ♩ = 94

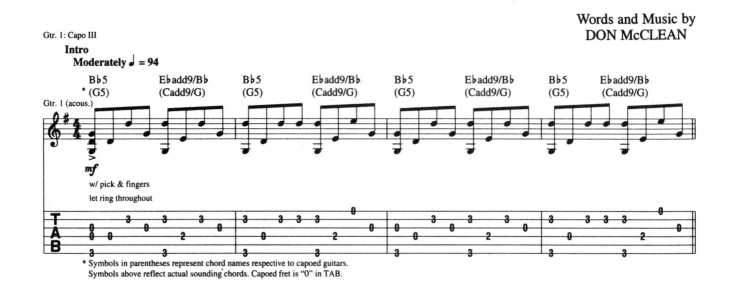

* Symbols in parentheses represent chord names respective to capoed guitars.
Symbols above reflect actual sounding chords. Capoed fret is "0" in TAB.

𝄋 Verse

1. And I love you so.
2. And you love me too.

The people ask me
Your thoughts are just for

** Chord symbols reflect overall tonality.

— how, — how I've lived 'til now.
— me. — You set my spir-it free.

And I Love You So - 5 - 1

⊕ *Coda*

AND IT STONED ME

Words and Music by
VAN MORRISON

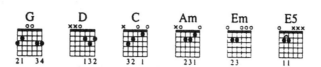

Moderately slow ♩ = 80

Verse :

1. Half a mile from the coun-ty fair, _ and the rain _ came _ pour-in' down. _
2. 3. *See additional lyrics*

Me and Bil-ly stand-in' there, _ with a sil-ver half-a-crown. _

Hands are full of a fish-in' rod, _ and the tack-le ___ on our backs.

We just stood _ there get-tin' wet _ with our backs a-gainst _ the fence.

Pre - Chorus :

Oh, ___ the wa-ter, oh, ___ the wa-ter,

Oh, ___ the wa-ter, hope it don't _ rain all day. _

And It Stoned Me - 3 - 1

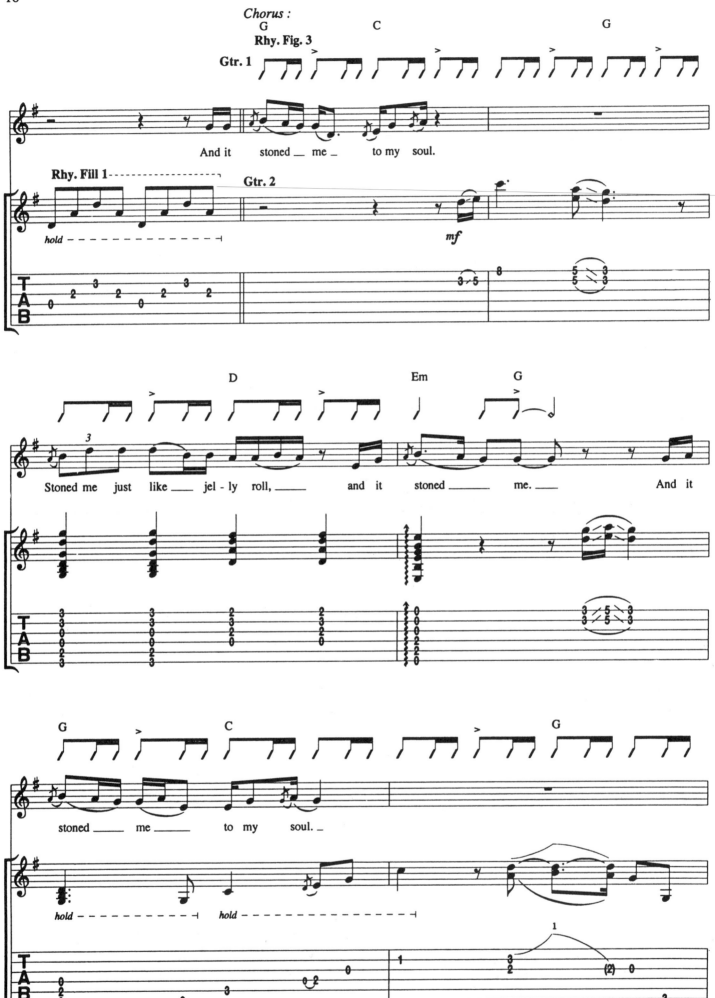

Verse 2:
Then the rain let up, and the sun came up and
We were gettin' dry.
Almost glad a pickup truck
Nearly passed us by.
So we jumped right in, and the driver grinned,
And he dropped us up the road.
And we looked at the swim,
And we jumped right in, not to mention fishing poles.
(To Pre - Chorus:)

Verse 3:
On the way back home we sang a song,
But our throats were getting dry.
Then we saw the man from across the road
With the sunshine in his eye.
Well, he lived alone, in his own little home,
With a great big gallon jar.
There were bottles two, one for me and you,
And he said, "Hey! There you are!"
(To Pre - Chorus:)

CAT'S IN THE CRADLE

Words and Music by
HARRY CHAPIN and SANDY CHAPIN

Moderately, with a 2 feel ♩ = 75

Intro:

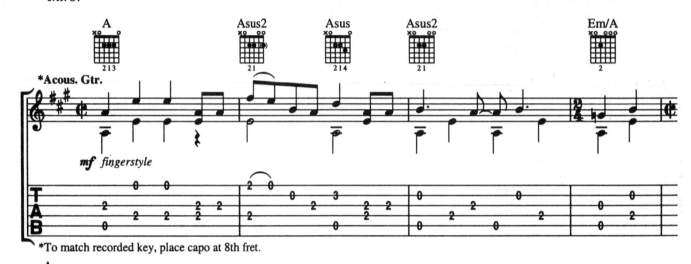

*To match recorded key, place capo at 8th fret.

1. My

Verses 1, 2, & 3:

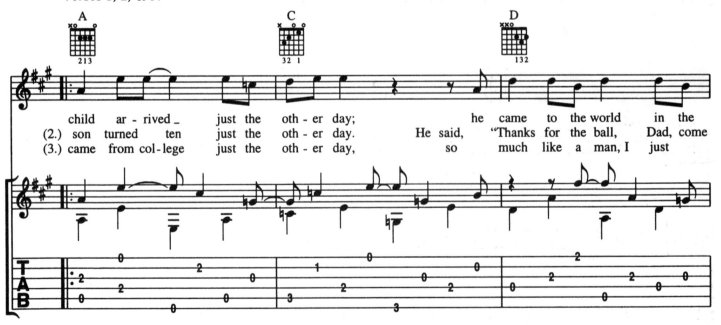

child ar - rived _ just the oth - er day;   he came to the world in the
(2.) son turned ten just the oth - er day.   He said, "Thanks for the ball, Dad, come
(3.) came from col - lege just the oth - er day,   so much like a man, I just

Cat's in the Cradle - 6 - 1

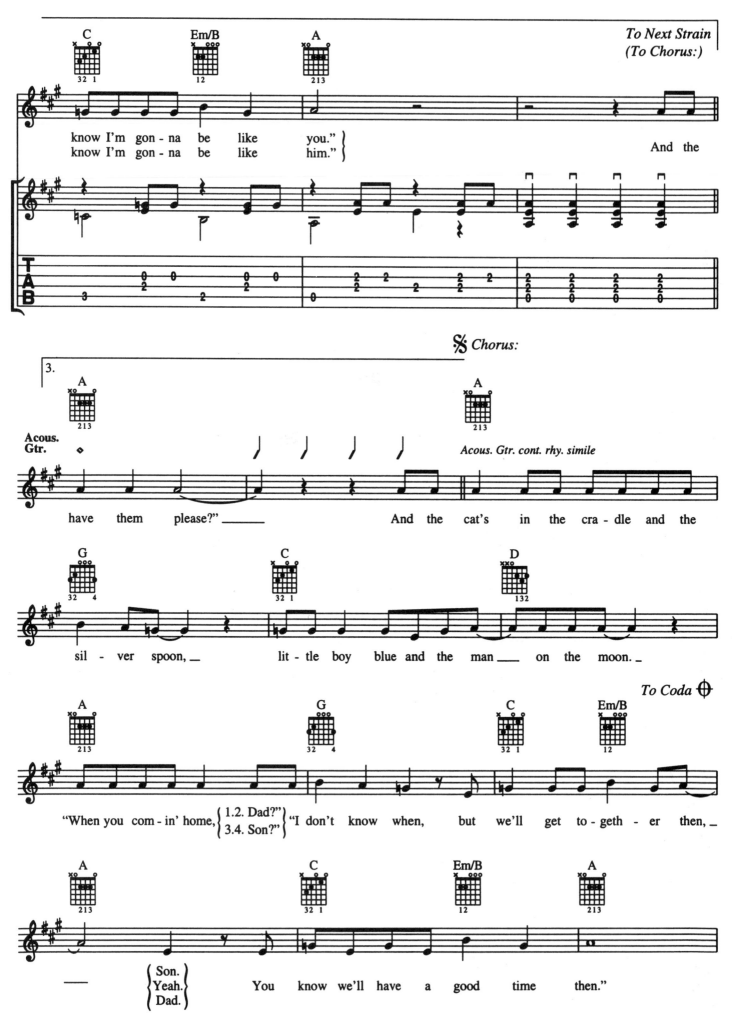

Verse 4:

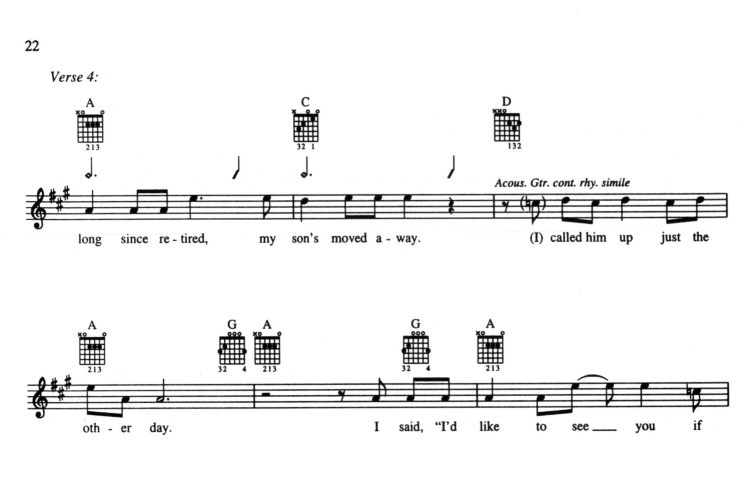

long since re - tired,   my son's moved a - way.   (I) called him up   just the

oth - er day.   I said, "I'd like   to see ____ you if

you don't mind." __ He said, "I'd love to, Dad, _ if I could find   the time.   You see, my

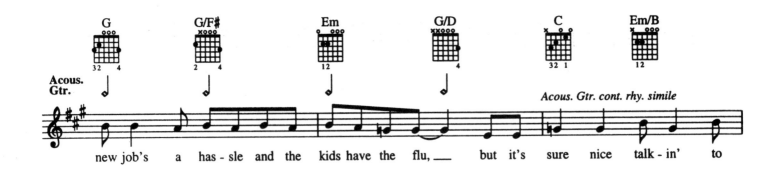

new job's   a has - sle and the kids have the flu, ___ but it's sure nice talk - in' to

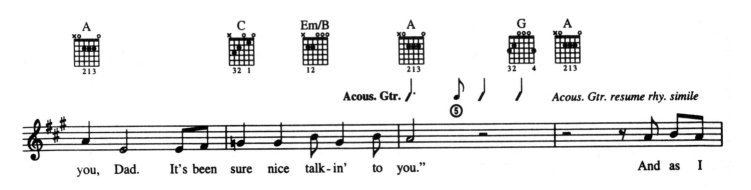

you, Dad. It's been sure nice talk - in' to you."   And as I

23

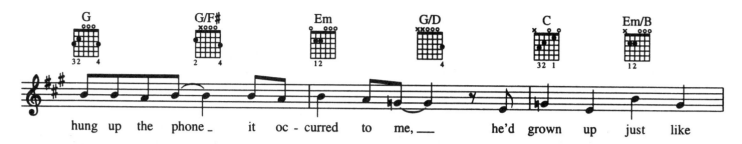

hung up the phone _ it oc - curred to me, __ he'd grown up just like

D.S. 𝄋 al Coda

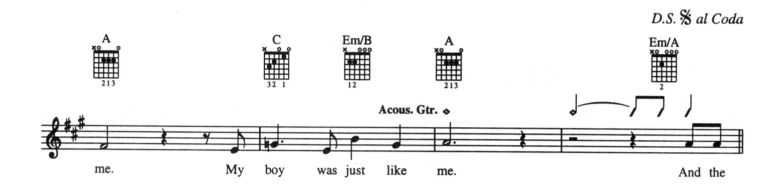

me. My boy was just like me. And the

Coda

A little slower

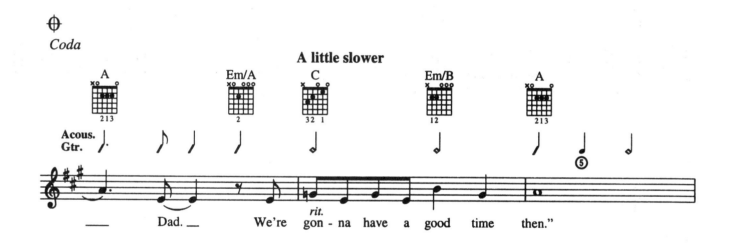

__ Dad. __ We're gon - na have a good time then."

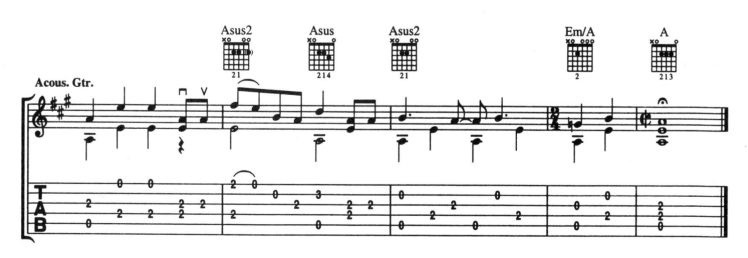

Cat's in the Cradle - 6 - 6

CALIFORNIA DREAMIN'

Words and Music by
JOHN PHILLIPS and MICHELLE PHILLIPS

Verse 2:
Stopped into a church
I passed along the way.
Well, I got down on my knees (Got down on my knees.)
And I pretend to pray. (I pretend to pray.)
You know the preacher liked the cold (Preacher liked the cold.)
He knows I'm gonna stay. (Knows I'm gonna stay.)
(To Chorus:)

Verse 3:
All the leaves are brown (All the leaves are brown)
And the sky is gray. (And the sky is gray.)
I've been for a walk (I've been for a walk)
On a winter's day. (On a winter's day.)
If I didn't tell her, (If I didn't tell her,)
I could leave today. (I could leave today.)
(To Chorus:)

BOTH SIDES, NOW

Words and Music by
JONI MITCHELL

Gtr. 1 Capo 2; tuning:

⑥ = E ③ = G#

⑤ = B ② = B

④ = E ① = E

Moderately ♩ = 98

Intro:

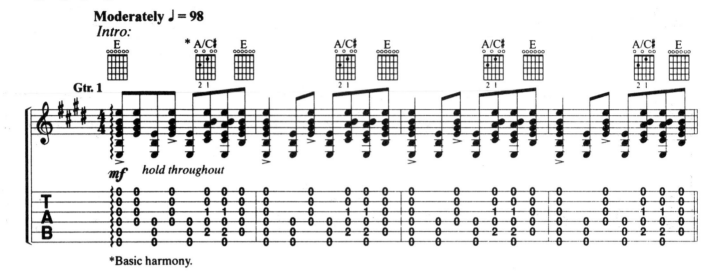

*Basic harmony.

Verses:

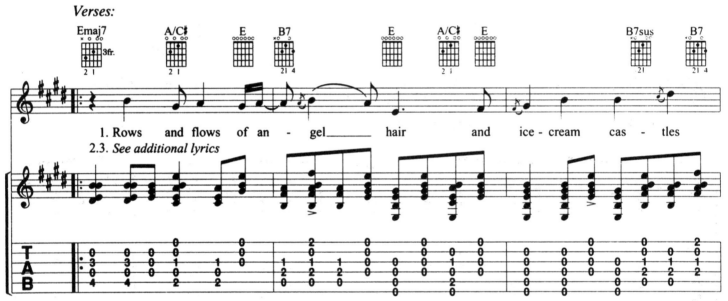

1. Rows and flows of an - gel_____ hair and ice-cream cas - tles
2.3. *See additional lyrics*

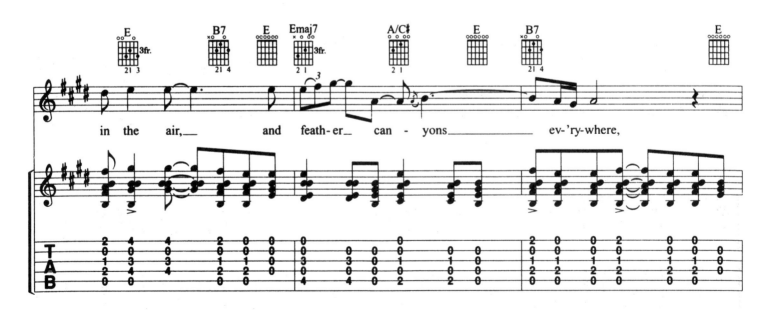

in the air,___ and feath-er__ can - yons_____ ev-'ry-where,

Both Sides, Now - 5 - 1

Both Sides, Now - 5 - 2

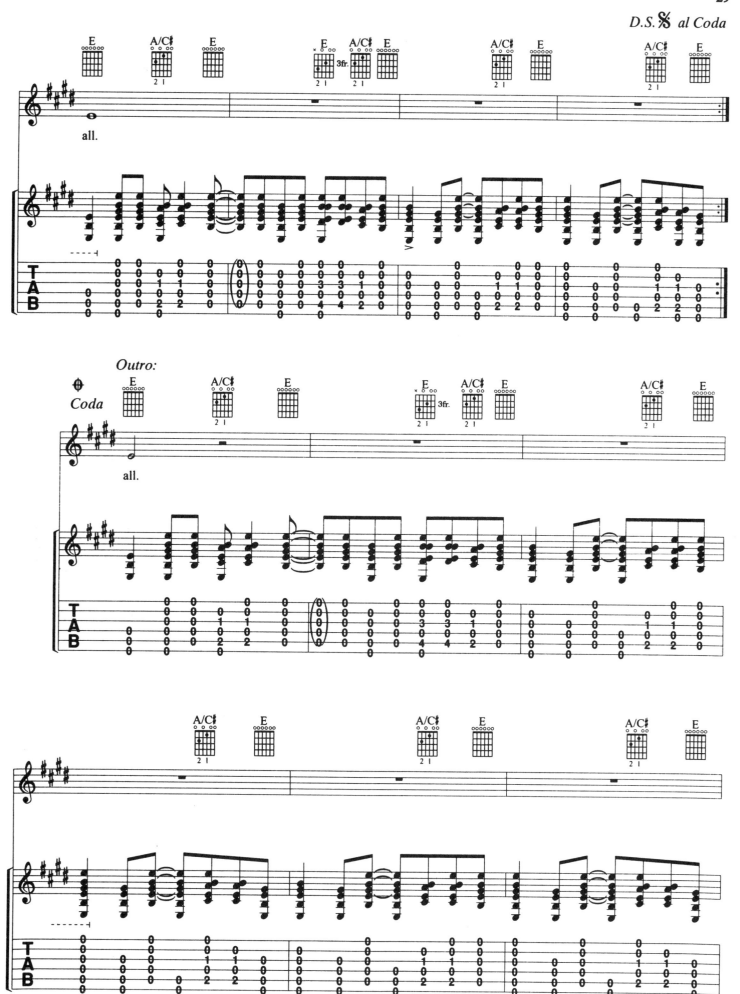

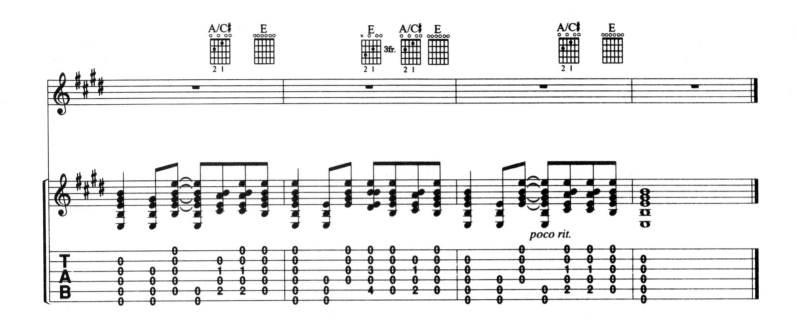

poco rit.

Verse 2:
Moons and Junes and Ferris wheels,
The dizzy dancing way you feel,
As every fairy tale comes real,
I've looked at love that way.
But now it's just another show,
You leave 'em laughing when you go.
And if you care, don't let them know,
Don't give yourself away.

Chorus 2:
I've looked at love from both sides now,
From give and take, and still, somehow
It's love's illusions I recall.
I really don't know love at all.

Verse 3:
Tears and fears and feeling proud,
To say "I love you" right out loud,
Dreams and schemes and circus crowds,
I've look at life that way.
But now old friends are acting strange,
They shake their heads, they say I've changed.
Well, something's lost but something's gained,
In living every day.

Chorus 3:
I've looked at life from both sides now,
From win and lose, and still, somehow
It's life's illusions I recall.
I really don't know life at all.

THE CIRCLE GAME

Gtr. 1 tune to and capo 4th fret:

⑥ = D	③ = G
⑤ = G	② = B
④ = D	① = D

Words and Music by
JONI MITCHELL

Moderately fast ♩ = 120

Intro:

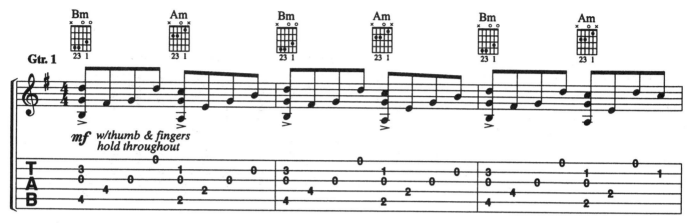

*Basic harmony.

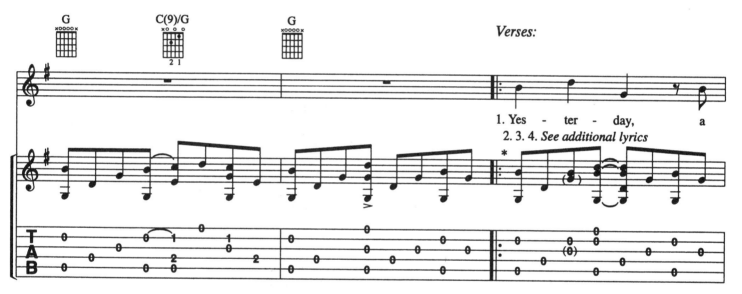

Verses:

1. Yes - ter - day, a
2. 3. 4. *See additional lyrics*

*Gtr. 1 dbld. by 2nd acoustic gtr.,
arranged here for one gtr.

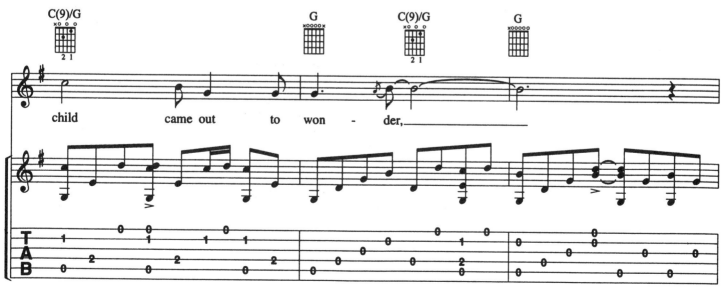

child   came out   to   won - der,_____

The Circle Game - 5 - 1

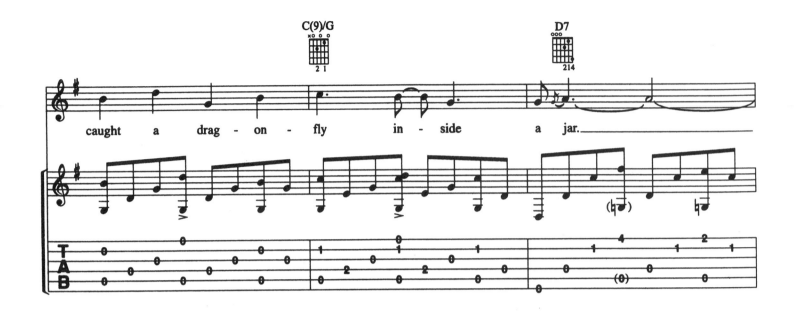

caught a drag - on - fly in - side a jar._____

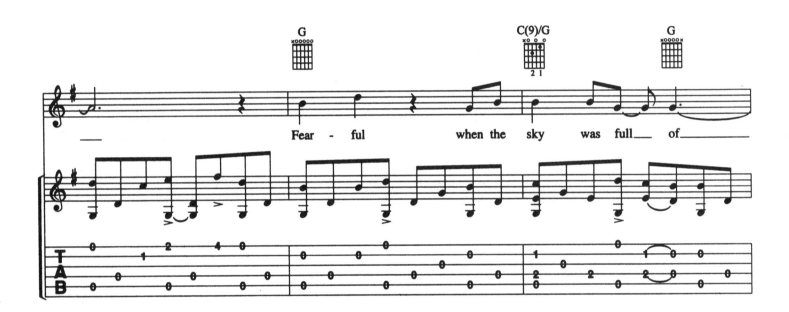

____ Fear - ful when the sky was full__ of_____

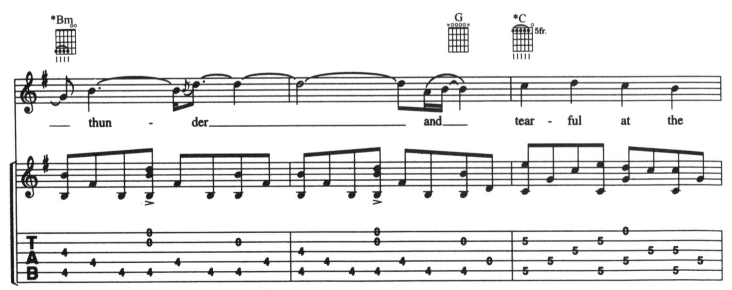

____ thun - der_____ and___ tear - ful at the

* Overhand barre. Reach left hand over neck.

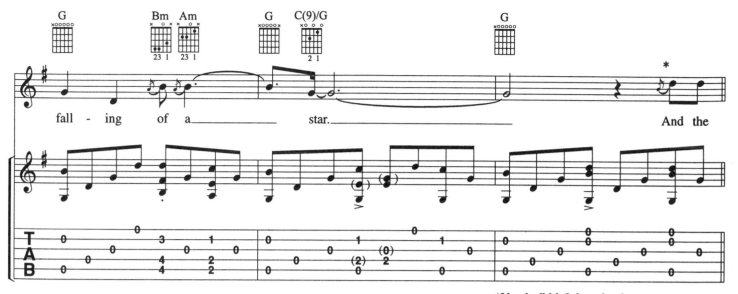

*Vocals dbld. 8vb and unison.

Chorus:

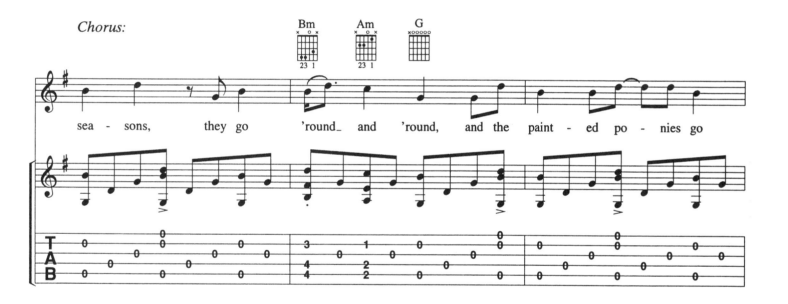

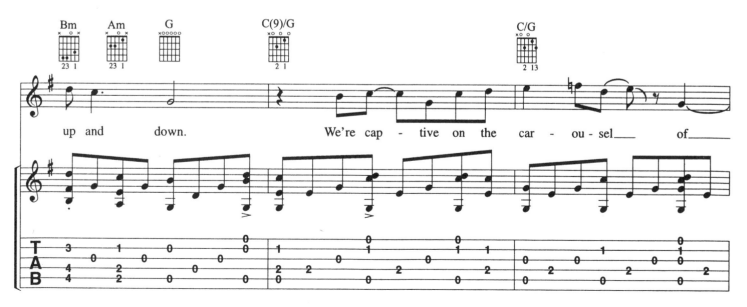

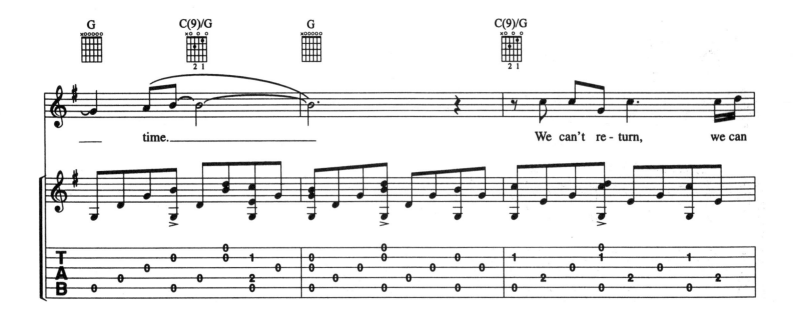

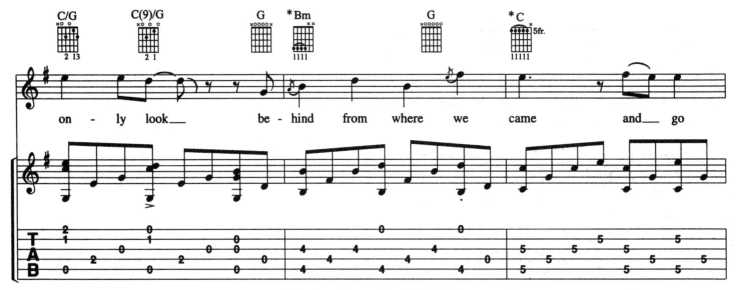

* Overhand barre. Reach left hand **over** neck.

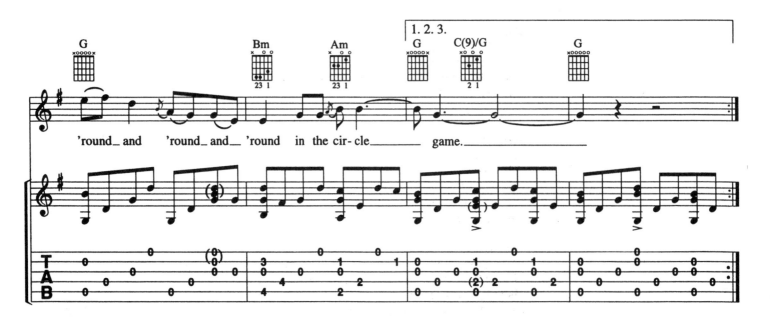

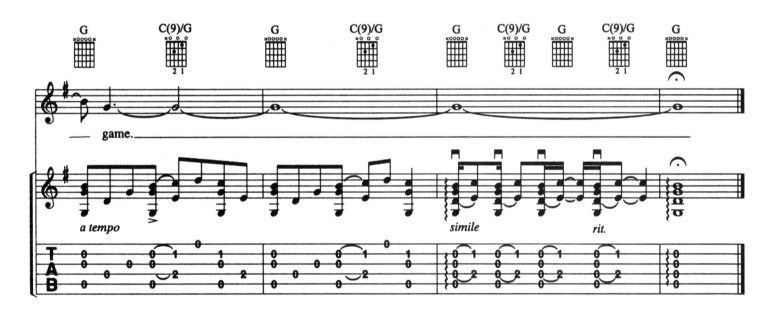

Verse 2:
Then the child moved ten times 'round the seasons,
Skated over ten clear frozen streams.
Words like, "When you're older," must appease him,
And promises of someday make his dreams...
(To Chorus:)

Verse 3:
Sixteen springs and sixteen summers gone now,
Cartwheels turn to car wheels through the town.
And they tell him, "Take your time, it won't be long now,
Till you drag your feet to slow the circles down"...
(To Chorus:)

Verse 4:
So the years spin by and now the boy is twenty;
Though his dreams have lost some grandeur coming true,
There'll be new dreams, maybe better dreams and plenty,
Before the last revolving year is through...
(To Chorus:)

CHELSEA MORNING

Words and Music by
JONI MITCHELL

1. Woke up,__ it was a Chel-sea morn-ing, and the first thing that I heard__ was a
2. Woke up,__ it was a Chel-sea morn-ing, and the first thing that I saw__ was the

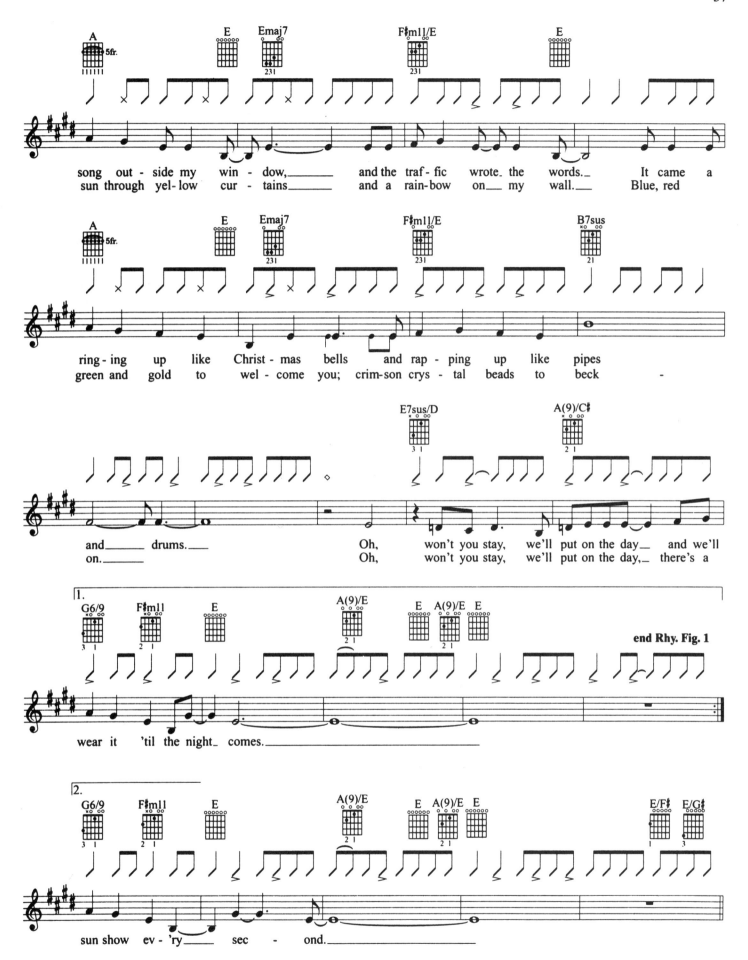

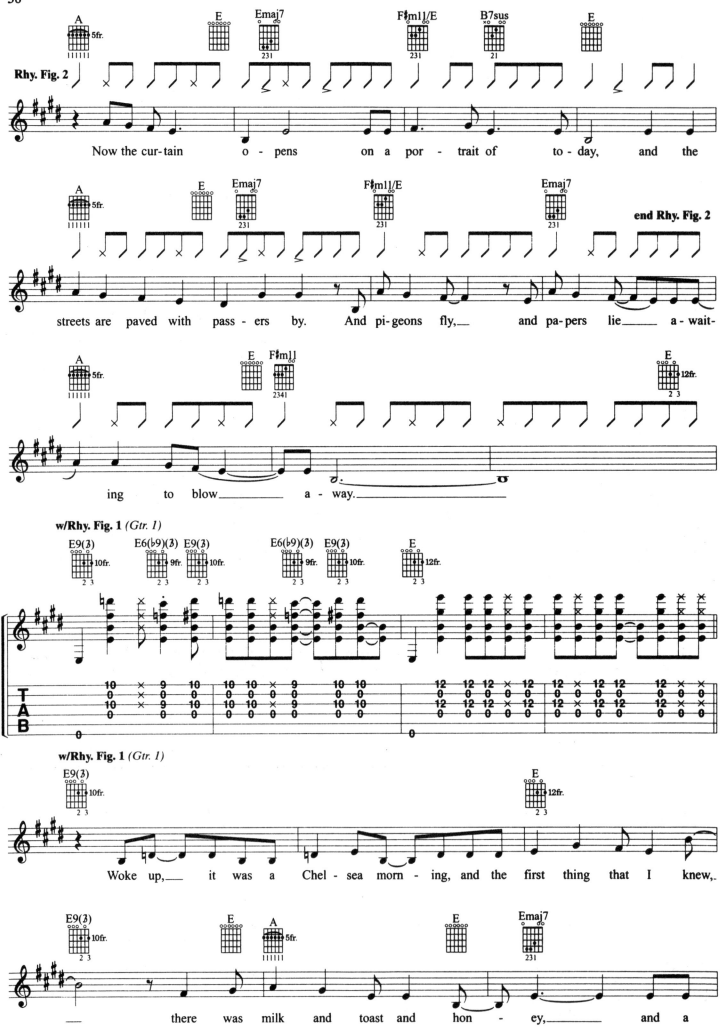

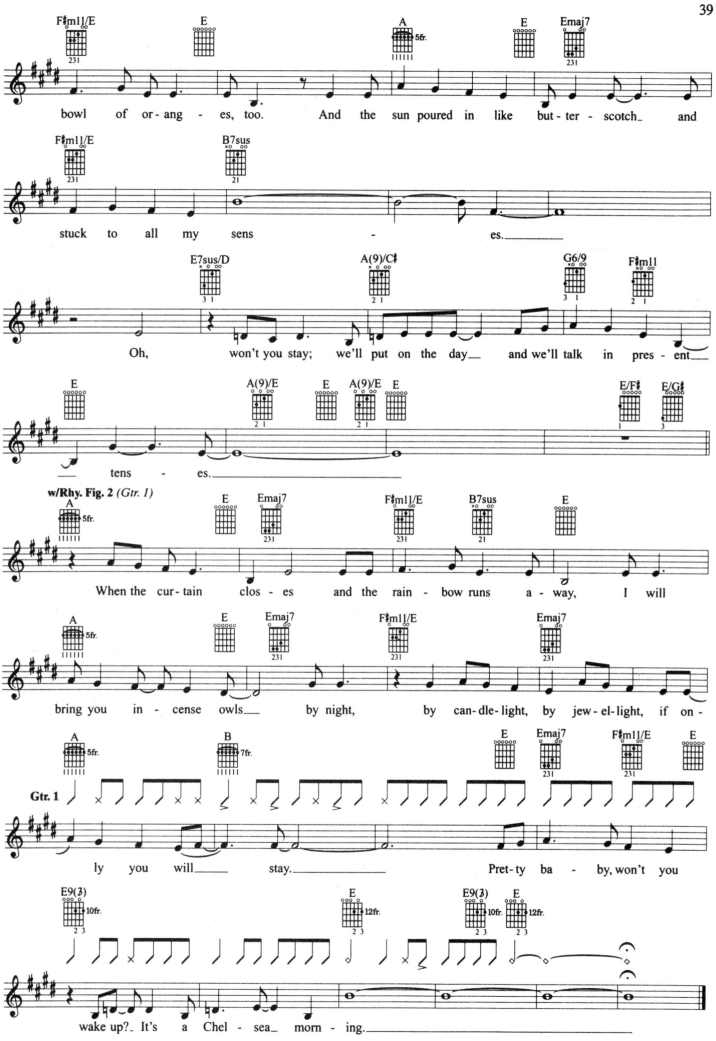

COPPERLINE

Words and Music by
JAMES TAYLOR and REYNOLDS PRICE

Slowly ♩ = 72
Intro:

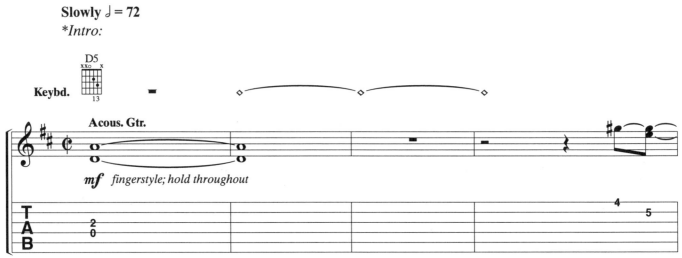

*Capo 2nd fret to match pitch of recording.

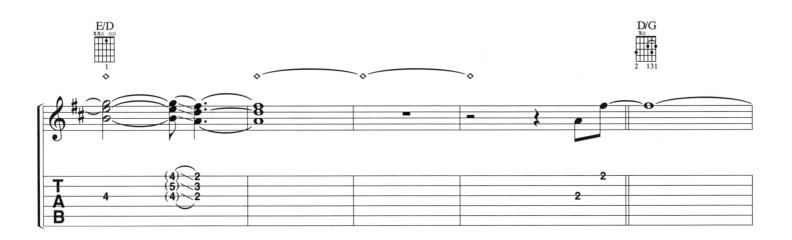

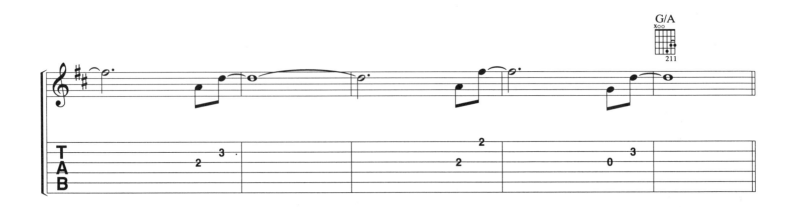

Copperline - 4 - 1

Verse 2:
Warm summer night on the Copperline,
Slip away past supper time.
Wood smoke and moonshine,
Down on Copperline.
One time I saw my daddy dance,
Watched him moving like a man in a trance.
He brought it back from the war in France,
Down on Copperline.

Bridge 2:
Branch water and tomato wine,
Creosote and turpentine.
Sour mash and new moonshine,
Down on Copperline,
We were down on Copperline.

Verse 3:
First kiss ever I took,
Like a page from a romance book.
The sky opened and the earth shook,
Down on Copperline,
Down on Copperline.
(To Guitar Solo:)

Bridge 3:
Took a fall from a windy height,
I only knew how to hold on tight,
And pray for love enough to last all night,
Down on Copperline.
(To Interlude:)

Verse 4:
I tried to go back, as if I could.
All spec house and plywood.
Tore up and tore up good,
Down on Copperline.
It doesn't come as a surprise to me,
It doesn't touch my memory.
Man, I'm lifting up and rising free,
Down over Copperline.

Bridge 4:
Half a mile down to Morgan Creek,
I'm only living for the end of the week.
Hercules and a hog-nosed snake,
Down on Copperline,
We were down on Copperline.
(To Outro:)

CRAZY LOVE

By
VAN MORRISON

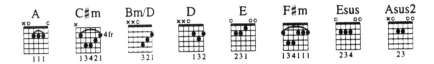

Moderately slow ♩ = 76

1. I can hear her heart beat from a thou-sand miles, and the

*Gtr. 1 (Acoustic) 2. 3. See additional lyrics

*Played fingerstyle throughout .

heav-ens o-pen ev-'ry time she smiles. And when I come to her that's

where I be-long, yet I'm run-ning to her like a riv-er's song. She give me

Crazy Love - 4 - 1

46

Crazy Love - 4 - 3

Verse 2 ·
She's got a fine sense of humor,
When I'm feeling low - down.
And when I come to her
When the sun goes down.
Take away my trouble,
Take away my grief,
Take away my heartache
In the night, like a thief.
(To Chorus :)

Verse 3 :
And when I'm returning from so far away,
She gives me some sweet lovin',
Brightens up my day.
Yeah, and it makes me righteous.
Yeah, and it makes me whole.
Yeah, and it makes me mellow
Down into my soul.
(To Chorus :)

CREEQUE ALLEY

Words and Music by
JOHN PHILLIPS and MICHELLE GILLIAM

Lyrics in score:

1. John and Mit-chie were get-tin' kind of itch-y just to leave the folk mu-sic be-hind.
2.3.4.6. *See additional lyrics*
5. *Flute Solo*

Zal and Den-ny, work-in' for a pen-ny, try'n' to get a fish on the line.

In a cof-fee house Se-bas-tian sat, and af-ter ev-'ry num-ber they passed the hat. Mc-Guinn and Mc-Guire's just a-get-tin' high-er in L.A., you know where that's at.

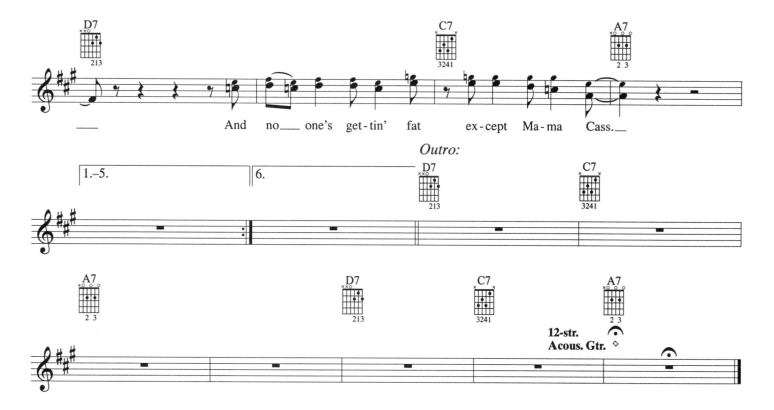

And no one's gettin' fat except Mama Cass.

Outro:

Verse 2:
Zally said, "Denny, you know there aren't many
Who can sing a song the way that you do."
"Let's go south." Denny said, "Zally, golly, don't you think that
I wish I could play guitar like you?"
Zal, Denny, and Sebastian sat, (at the Night Owl)
And after every number they passed the hat.
McGuinn and McGuire still are gettin' higher in L. A.,
You know where that's at.
And no one's gettin' fat except Mama Cass.

Verse 3:
When Cass was a sophomore, planned to go to Swarthmore,
But she changed her mind one day.
Standin' on the turnpike, thumb out to hitchhike,
Take her to New York right away.
When Denny met Cass, he gave her love bumps,
Called John and Zal and that was the Mugwumps.
McGuinn and McGuire couldn't get no higher
But that's what they were aimin' at.
And no one's gettin' fat except Mama Cass.

Verse 4:
Mugwumps, high jumps, low slumps, big bumps,
Don't you work as hard as you play?
Make-up, break-up, everything you shake up,
Guess it had to be that way.
Sebastian and Zal formed the Spoonful,
Michelle, John, and Denny gettin' very tuneful.
McGuinn and McGuire, just a-catchin' fire in L.A.,
You know where that's at.
And everybody's gettin' fat except Mama Cass.
(To Flute Solo:)

Verse 6:
Broke, busted, disgusted, agents can't be trusted,
And then she wants to go to the sea.
Cass can't make it, she says, "We'll have to fake it."
We knew she'd come eventually.
Greasin' on American Express cards, tents, low rent,
But keepin' out the heat's hard.
Duffy's good vibrations and our imaginations
Can't go on indefinitely.
And California dreamin' is becoming a reality.

DAYS LIKE THESE

Words and Music by
JANIS IAN

*Brush down w/right-hand
fingernails on accents.

days like these, when the rain won't _ fall _ and the sky is so dry _ that e - ven

2.3. *See additional lyrics*

birds can't _ call, I can feel your tears _ dis - ap - pear - ing in the

To Coda

air car - ried on the _ breeze in days like these. _

_____ 2. It's _____ But you can't _

Days Like These - 2 - 1

Verse 2:
It's years like these that make a young man old
Bend his back against the promises that life should hold
They can make him wise, they can drive him to his knees
Nothin' comes for free in days like these.

Verse 3:
In lives like these, when ev'ry moment counts,
I add up all the things that I can live without.
When one thing left is the placing of my dreams,
Then I can make my peace with days like these.
I can make my peace with days like these.

Days Like These – 2 – 2

COME MONDAY

Gtr. 2 (Capo 7)

Words and Music by
JIMMY BUFFET

Moderately ♩ = 100
Intro:

*Gtr. 2 is capoed at the 7th fret.
Chord grids indicate Gtr. 1 w/o capo.

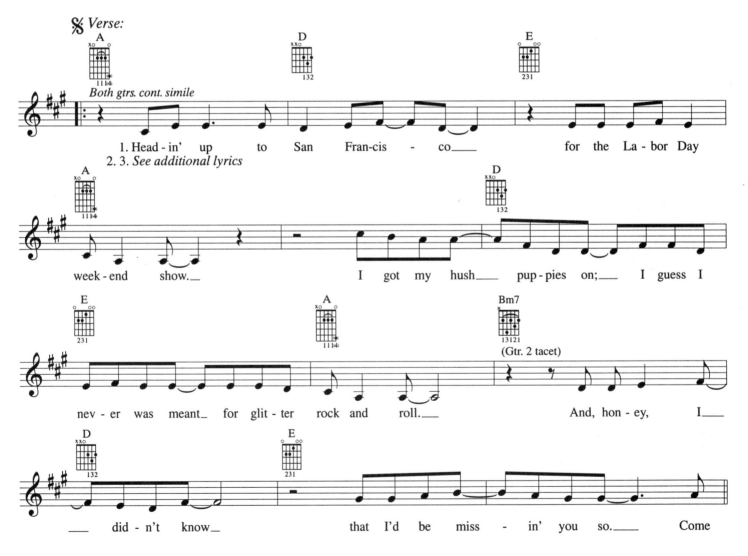

Verse:

Both gtrs. cont. simile

1. Head-in' up to San Fran-cis-co___ for the La-bor Day
2. 3. *See additional lyrics*

week-end show.___ I got my hush___ pup-pies on;___ I guess I

(Gtr. 2 tacet)

nev-er was meant_ for glit-ter rock and roll.___ And, hon-ey, I___

___ did-n't know_ that I'd be miss-in' you so.___ Come

Come Monday - 3 - 1

D.S. % al Coda

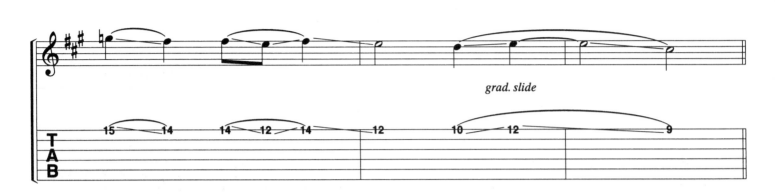

grad. slide

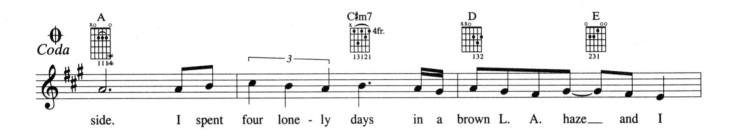

Coda

side.   I spent four lone - ly days   in a brown L. A. haze___ and I

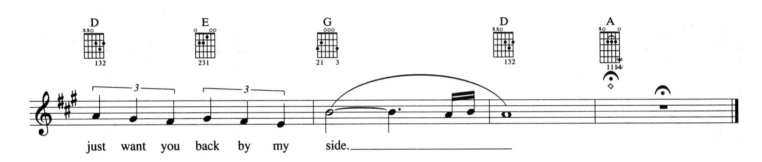

just want you back by my side._____

Verse 2:
Yes, it's been quite a summer,
Rent-a-cars and westbound trains,
And now you're off on vacation.
Somethin' you tried to explain.
And, darlin', it's I love you so,
That's the reason I just let you go.
(To Chorus:)

Verse 3:
I hope you're enjoyin' the scen'ry,
I know that it's pretty up there.
We can go hikin' on Tuesday,
With you I'd walk anywhere.
California has worn me quite thin,
I just can't wait to see you again.
(To Chorus:)

EARLY MORNIN' RAIN

All gtrs. capo 1st fret.

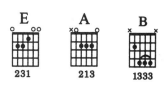

Words and Music by
GORDON LIGHTFOOT

Moderately fast in 2 ♩ = 106

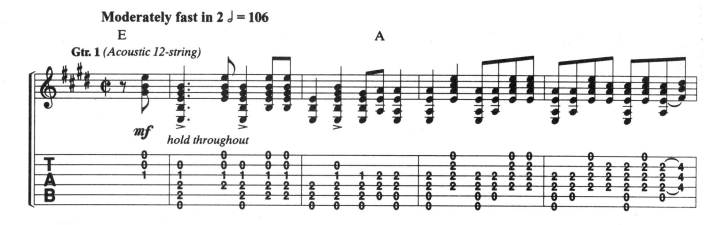

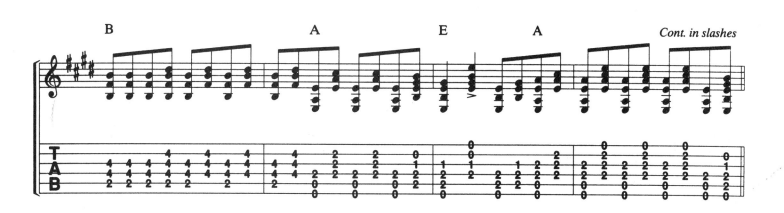

Verses:

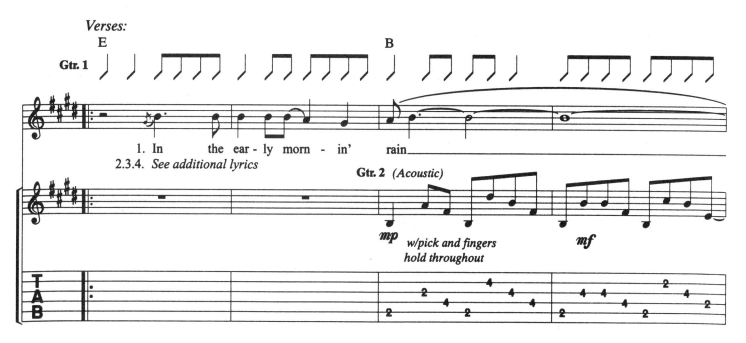

1. In the ear-ly morn-in' rain _____
2.3.4. *See additional lyrics*

mp
w/pick and fingers
hold throughout
mf

Early Mornin' Rain - 5 - 1

Early Mornin' Rain - 5 - 4

Verse 2:

Out on runway number nine,
Big 707 set to go,
But I'm stuck here in the grass
Where the pavement never grows.
Now, the liquor tasted good,
And the women all were fast,
Well, there she goes, my friend,
She'll be rollin' down at last.

Verse 3:

Hear the mighty engines roar,
See the silver bird on high,
She's away and westward bound,
Far above the clouds she'll fly
Where the mornin' rain don't fall
And the sun always shines,
She'll be flyin' over my home
In about three hours time.

Verse 5:

This old airport's got me down,
It's no earthly good to me,
And I'm stuck here on the ground
As cold and drunk as I can be.
You can't jump a jet plane
Like you can a freight train.
So, I'd best be on my way
In the early mornin' rain.

Early Mornin' Rain - 5 - 5

FEARLESS HEART

Words and Music by
STEVE EARLE

1. Don't you wor - ry 'bout what you've been told,____
2. Folks will tell you that I'm just no good,____
3. *See additional lyrics*

'cause, hon - ey, I____ ain't e - ven close____ to cold.____
but I would - n't hurt you, hon - ey, if I____ could.____

Fearless Heart - 3 - 1

It's kind-a soon to fall in love____ a-gain.____
Now, I can't prom-ise this-'ll work out right,____

Some-times the best that you can do is just jump back in.____
but it would kill me, dar-ling, if we did-n't e-ven try.____

Chorus:

____ } I got me a fear-less heart,

strong e-nough to get you through the scar-y part.____

It's been bro-ken man-y times__ be-fore.____ A fear-less heart just comes

1.
back for more.____

D.S. % 3.
back for more.____

2.4.
back for more.____

Pedal-steel

Elec. 12-string *(arranged for 6-string gtr.)*

mp ———————— *mf*

1/2 1/2 1/2

Verse 3:
I admit I fall in love a lot,
But I nearly always give it my best shot.
I know you must think, I'm the reckless kind,
But I want a lady with a fearless heart,
Just like mine.
(To Chorus:)

GOOD OL' BOY
(Gettin' Tough)

Words and Music by
STEVE EARLE and RICHARD BENNETT

Good Ol' Boy (Gettin' Tough) - 5 - 1

64

Good Ol' Boy (Gettin' Tough) - 5 - 3

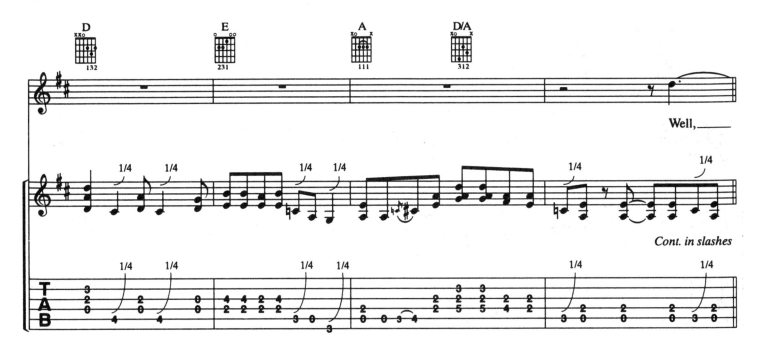

Well,____

Cont. in slashes

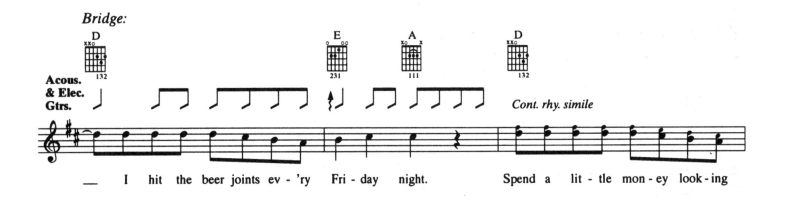

Bridge:

Acous.
& Elec.
Gtrs.

Cont. rhy. simile

___ I hit the beer joints ev - 'ry Fri - day night.   Spend a lit - tle mon - ey look - ing

for   a   fight.   It don't mat - ter if I   lose   or   win,__

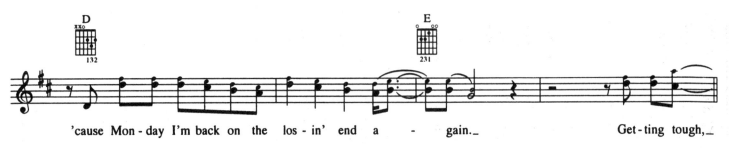

'cause Mon - day I'm back on the los - in' end a - gain.__   Get - ting tough,__

Good Ol' Boy (Gettin' Tough) - 5 - 4

Good Ol' Boy (Gettin' Tough) - 5 - 5

FIRST CUT IS THE DEEPEST

Words and Music by
CAT STEVENS

First Cut Is the Deepest - 2 - 1

HARVEST MOON

Words and Music by
NEIL YOUNG

Harvest Moon - 6 - 1

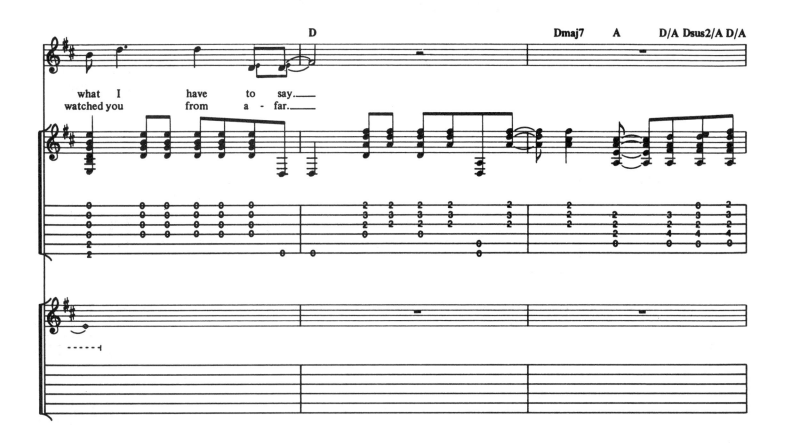

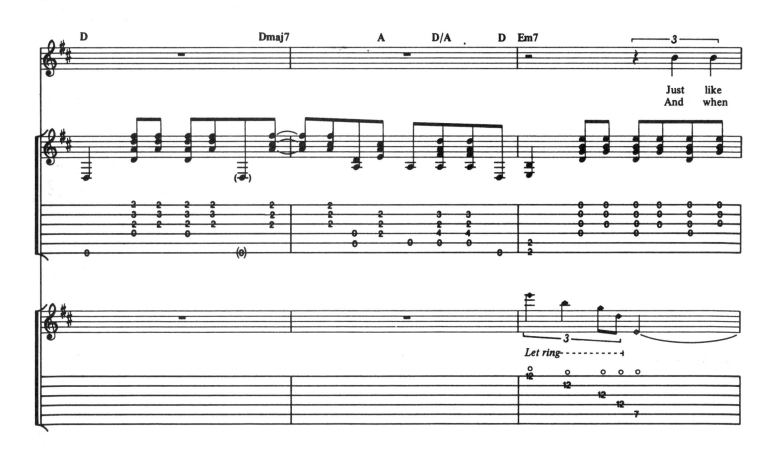

Harvest Moon - 6 - 2

Harvest Moon - 6 - 6

HEART OF GOLD

Words and Music by
NEIL YOUNG

Heart of Gold - 9 - 1

Heart of Gold - 9 - 3

Keep me search - in for a Heart of__ Gold,_____ an' I'm get -tin' old.__

Voice tacet
Instrumental (w/harmonica)

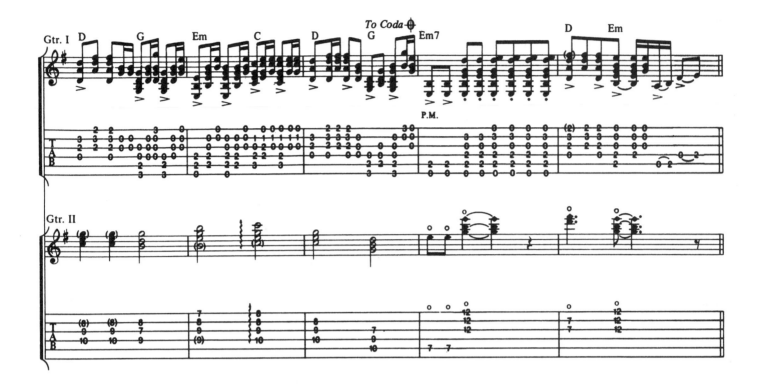

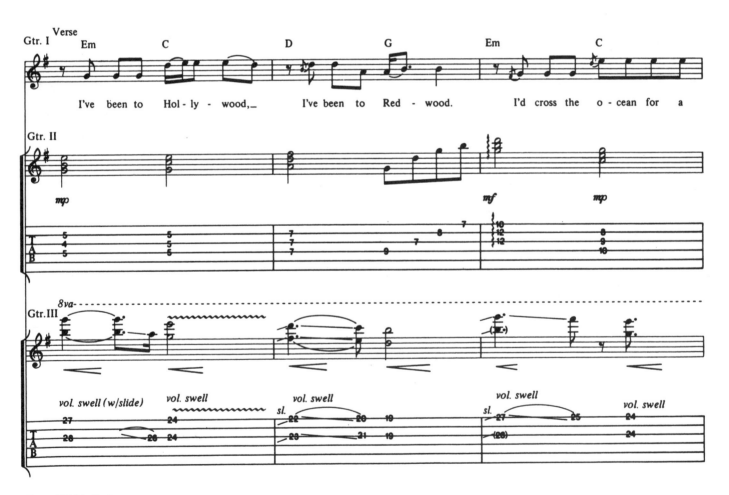

82

Heart of Gold - 9 - 7

Coda

Keep me search - in' for a Heart of Gold.____

You keep me search - in' an' I'm grow - in' old.____ Keep me search - in' for a

A HORSE WITH NO NAME

Words and Music by
DEWEY BUNNELL

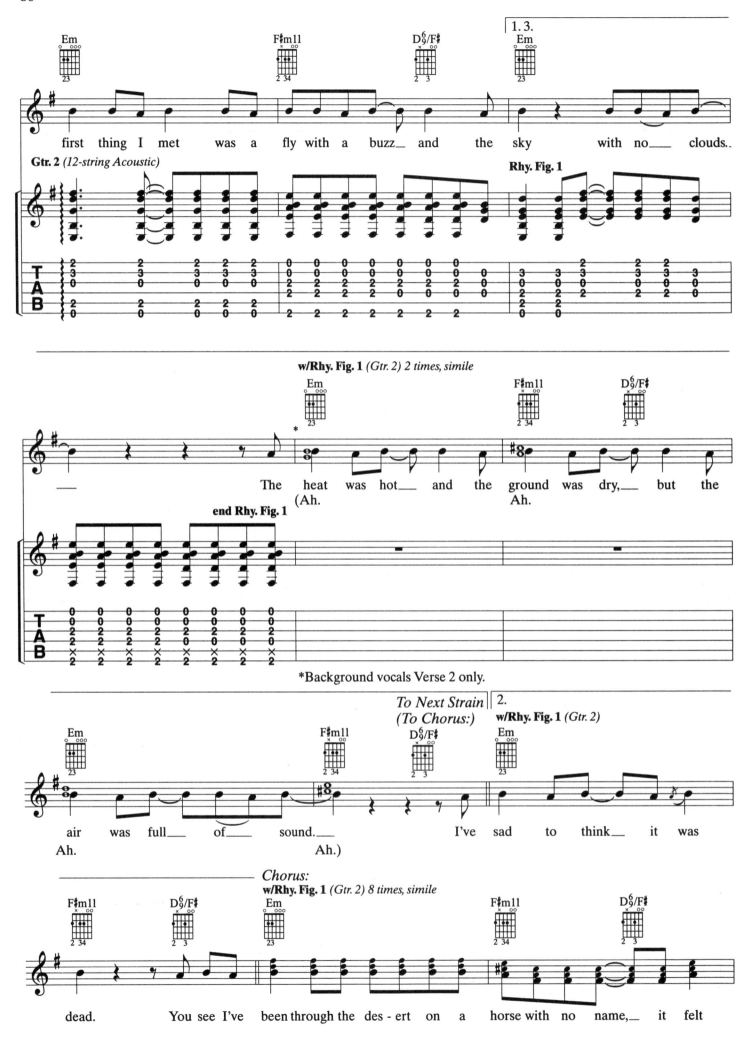

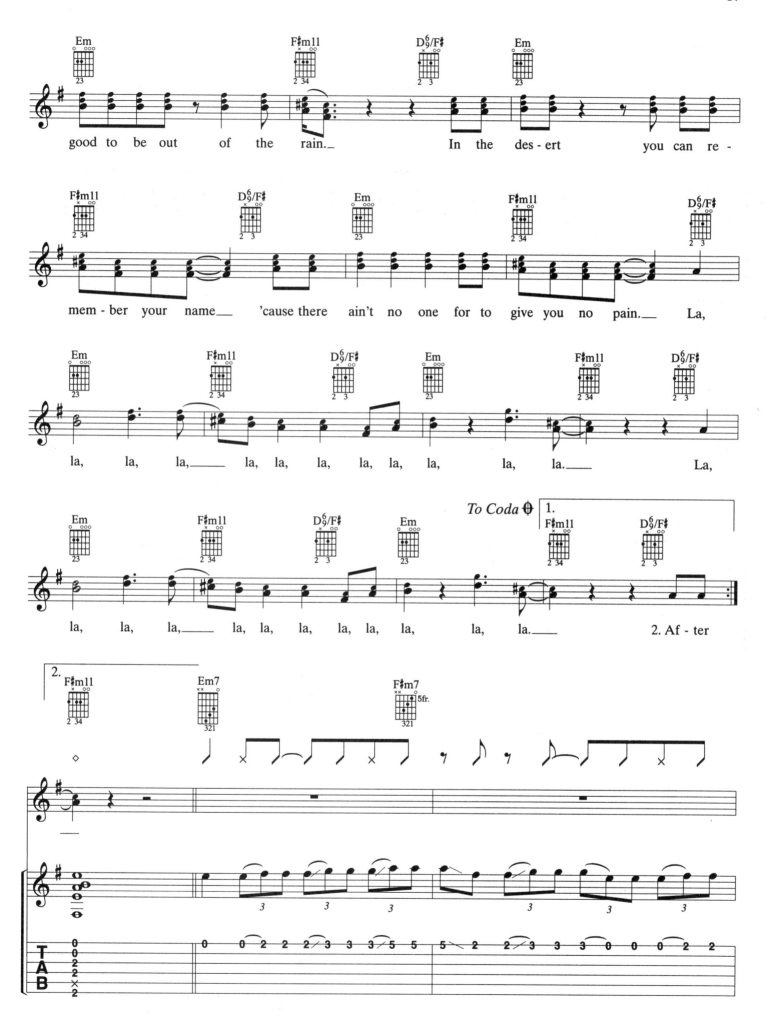

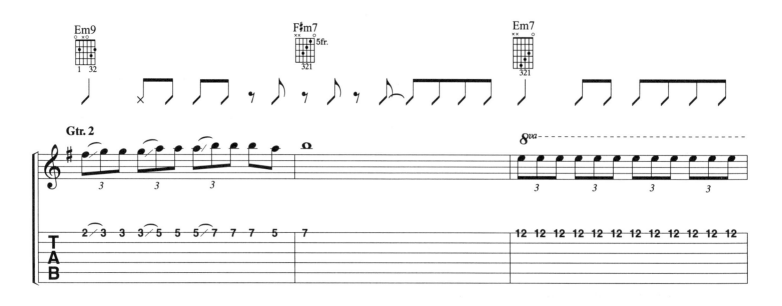

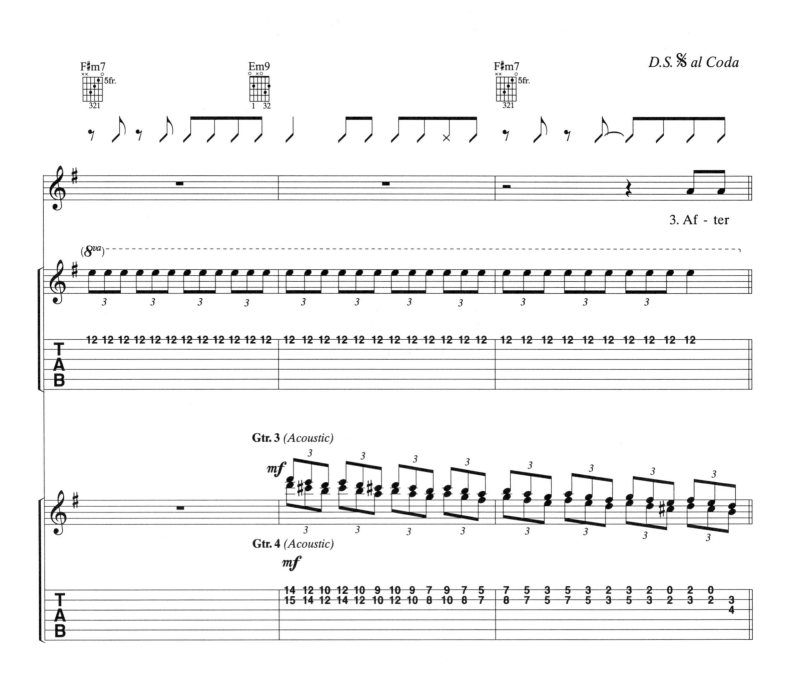

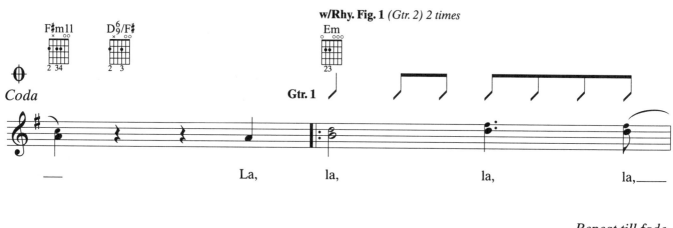

Coda

La, la, la, la,___

Repeat till fade

Cont. rhy. simile

___ la, la, la, la, la, la, la, la.___ La,

Verse 2:
After two days in the desert sun,
My skin began to turn red.
After three days in the desert fun,
I was looking at a river bed.
And the story it told of a river that flowed
Made me sad to think it was dead.
(To Chorus:)

Verse 3:
After nine days I let the horse run free
'Cause the desert had turned to sea.
There were plants and birds and rocks and things,
There was sand and hills and rings.
The ocean is a desert with its life underground
And a perfect disguise above.
Under the cities lies a heart made of ground,
But the humans will give no love.
(To Chorus:)

HOUSE AT POOH CORNER

Words and Music by
KENNY LOGGINS

w/Rhy. Fig. 2 *(Gtrs. 1 & 2)*

La la la la___ la___ la___ la la la.___ La la la la___ la la.___

w/Rhy. Fig. 1 *(Gtrs. 1 & 2)*

D.S. 𝄋 al Coda

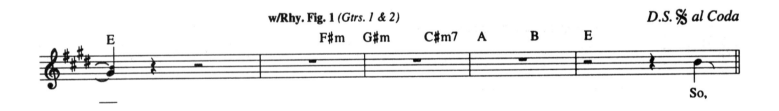

So,

Coda

Back to the days___ of Chris-to-pher___ Rob - in. Back to the ways___ of
way.___ Back to the day.___

Repeat and fade

Verse 2:
Winnie the Pooh doesn't know what to do,
Got a honey jar stuck on his nose.
He came to me asking help and advice,
And from here, no one knows where he goes.

Pre-Chorus 2:
So, I sent him to ask of the owl, if he's there,
How to loosen a jar from the nose of a bear.
(To Chorus:)

I LOVE MY DOG

Words and Music by
CAT STEVENS

Moderately ♩ = 92
Intro:

Verses 1 & 2:
w/Rhy. Fig. 1 *(Nylon-String Gtr.)*

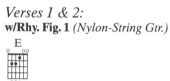

Acous. Gtr. cont. rhy. simile

love   my___ dog   as much as   I   love___ you.   But
love   my___ dog   as much as   I   love___ you.   But

I Love My Dog - 3 - 1

IF YOU COULD READ MY MIND

Gtr. 1 capo 2nd fret.

Words and Music by
GORDON LIGHTFOOT

Moderately fast ♩ = 120

Intro:

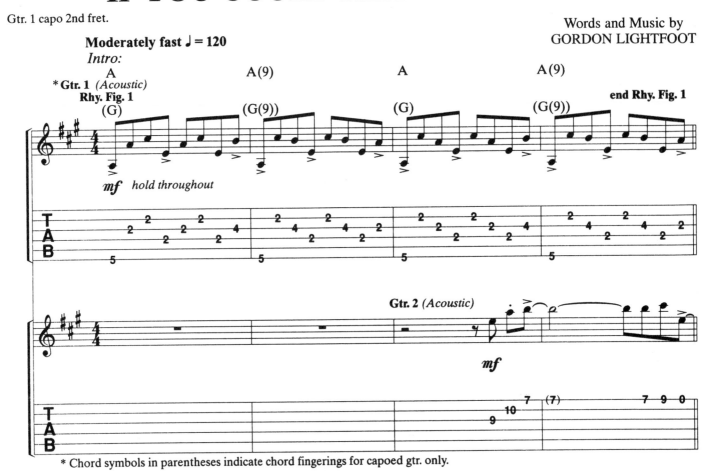

* Chord symbols in parentheses indicate chord fingerings for capoed gtr. only.

Verses:

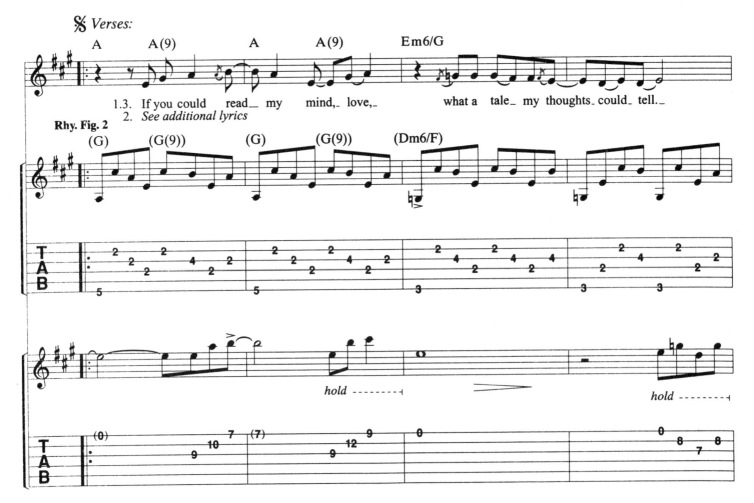

If You Could Read My Mind - 6 - 1

If You Could Read My Mind - 6 - 2

102

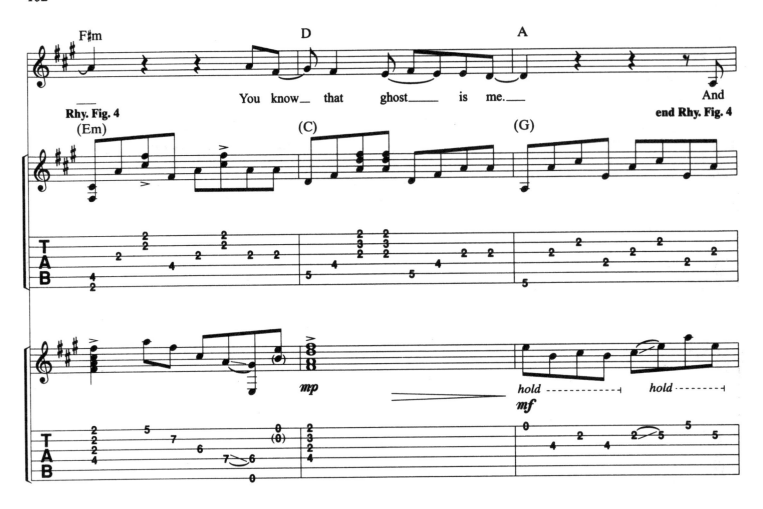

If You Could Read My Mind - 6 - 3

that you can't see.

end Rhy. Fig. 5

w/Rhy. Fig. 2 *(Gtr. 1) simile*

Gtr. 2

mp

mf

If You Could Read My Mind - 6 - 4

Bridge:

Verse 2:
If I could read your mind, love,
What a tale your thoughts could tell.
Just like a paperback novel,
The kind the drugstore sells.
When you reach the part where the heartaches come,
The hero would be me.
But heroes often fail.
And you won't read that book again
Because the ending's just too hard to take.

If You Could Read My Mind - 6 - 6

LYIN' EYES

Words and Music by
DON HENLEY and GLENN FREY

Lyin' Eyes - 5 - 1

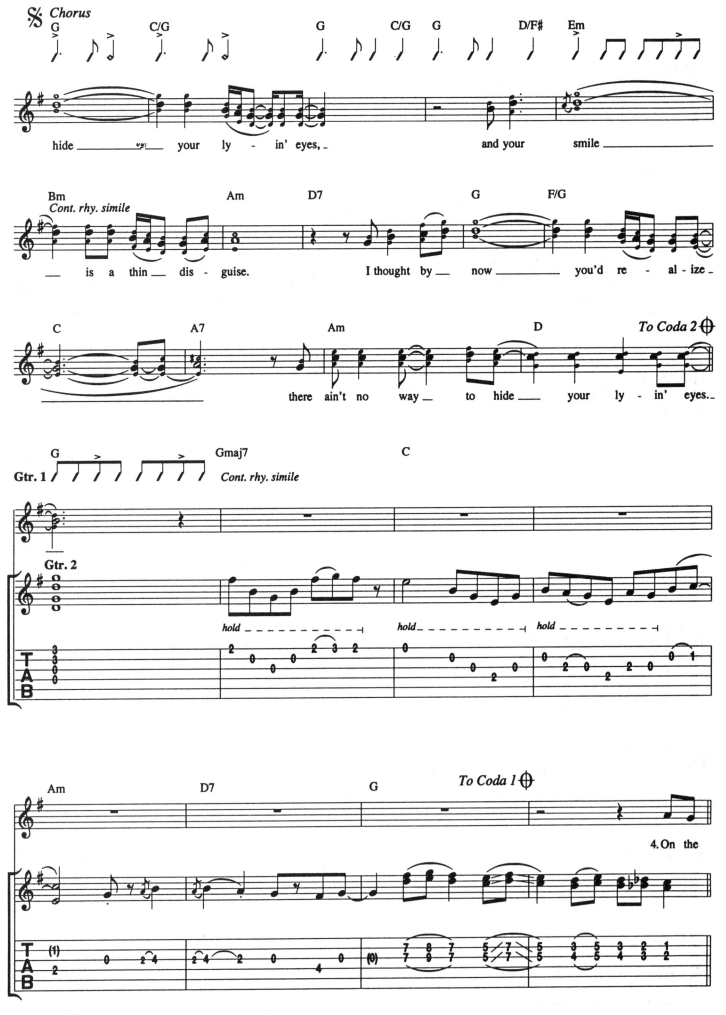

Verse 2:
Late at night her big old house gets lonely.
I guess every form of refuge has its price.
And it breaks her heart to think her love is only
Given to a man with hands as cold as ice.
(To Verse 3:)

Verse 5:
She rushes to his arms, they fall together.
She whispers that it's only for a while.
She swears that soon she'll be comin' back forever.
She pulls away and leaves him with a smile.
(To Chorus:)

Verse 7:
She wonders how it ever got so crazy.
She thinkgs about a boy she knew in school.
Did she get tired or did she just get lazy?
She's so far gone, she feels just like a fool.

Verse 8:
My oh my, you sure know how to arrange things.
You set it up so well—so carefully.
Ain't it funny how your new life didn't change things;
You're still the same girl you used to be.
(To Chorus:)

MR. BOJANGLES

Words and Music by
JERRY JEFF WALKER

Mr. Bojangles - 3 - 1

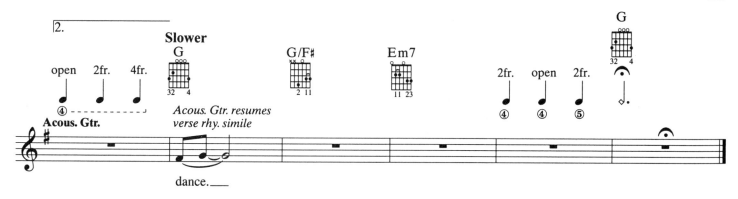

dance.___

Verse 2:
I met him in a cell in New Orleans.
I was down and out.
He looked to me to be
The eyes of age
As he spoke right out.
He talked of life.
He talked of life.
He laughed, clicked his heels and stepped.

Verse 3:
He said his name, "Bojangles," and he danced a lick
Across the cell.
He grabbed his pants and spread his stance,
Woah, he jumped so high
And then he clicked his heels.
He let go a laugh.
He let go a laugh,
Shook back his clothes all around.

Verse 4:
He danced for those in minstrel shows and county fairs
Throughout the South.
He spoke through tears of fifteen years,
How his dog and him
Travelled about.
The dog up and died.
He up and died.
After twenty years, he still grieves.

Verse 5:
He said, "I've danced now
At every chance in honky tonk
For drinks and tips.
But most the time was spent behind these county bars
'Cause I drinks a bit."
He shook his head.
And as he shook his head,
I heard someone ask him, "Please, please"…

MILLWORKER

Music and Lyrics by
JAMES TAYLOR

Millworker - 6 - 2

118

Millworker - 6 - 6

MY SWEET LADY

Words and Music by
JOHN DENVER

Verse 2:
Lady, are you happy?
Do you feel the way I do?
Are there meanings that you've never seen before?
Lady, my sweet lady,
I just can't believe it's true.
And it's like I've never ever loved before.
(To Bridge:)

A PIRATE LOOKS AT FORTY

Words and Music by
JIMMY BUFFETT

A Pirate Looks at Forty - 5 - 1

Acoustic gtr. same as verse 1
Elec. Gtr. (1st time only)

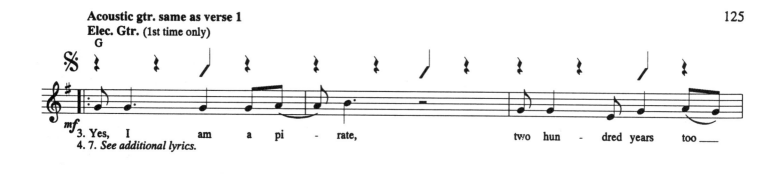

mf 3. Yes, I am a pi - rate, two hun - dred years too ___
4. 7. *See additional lyrics.*

late. The can - nons don't thun - der, there's noth - in' to plun - der, I'm an

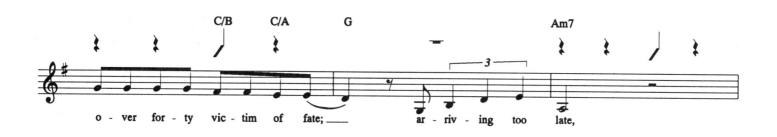

o - ver for - ty vic - tim of fate; ___ ar - riv - ing too late,

To Coda ⊕ *D.S.S.* 𝄋𝄋 *al Coda*

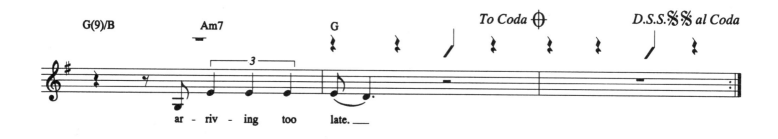

ar - riv - ing too late. ___

Acoustic gtr. same as other verses

5. I have been drunk ___ now for o - ver two weeks, I passed out and I ral - lied and I

sprung a few leaks, but I've got to stop wish - in', got to go fish - in', I'm down ___

A Pirate Looks at Forty - 5 - 3

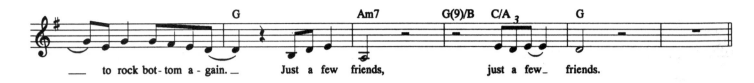

to rock bot-tom a-gain. Just a few friends, just a few friends.

Gtr. solo:
Acoustic gtr. continue simile

6. *(Instrumental)*

Marimba arr. for gtr.

Piano arr. for gtr.

D.S. 𝄋

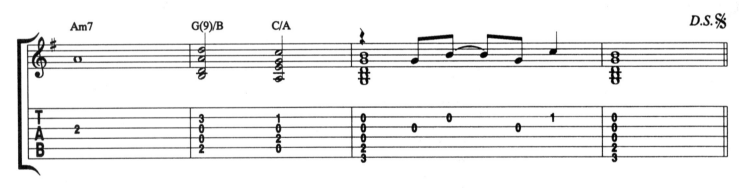

Coda

I feel like I've drowned, gon-na head up

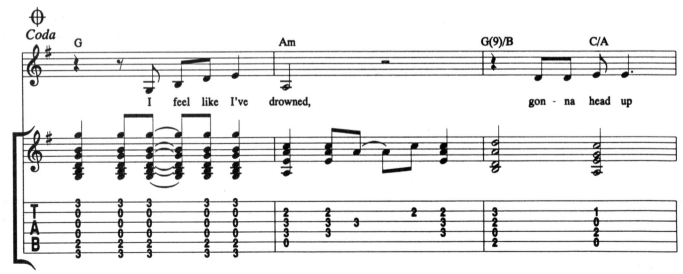

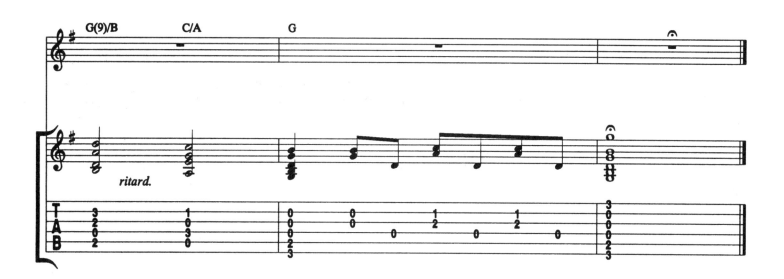

Verse 2:

Watched the men who rode you,
Switch from sails to steam.
And in your belly you hold the treasure
That few have ever seen. Most of them dreams,
Most of them dreams.

Verse 4:

I've done a bit of smugglin'.
I've run my share of grass.
I made enough money to buy Miami,
But I pissed it away so fast. Never meant to last,
Never meant to last.

Verse 6:
(Instrumental)

Verse 7:

I go for younger women,
Lived with several awhile,
And though I ran away, they'll come back one day,
And still I can manage a smile.
It just takes awhile, just takes awhile.

Verse 8:

Mother, mother ocean, after all these years I've found
My occupational hazard being my occupation's just not around.
I feel like I've drowned,
Gonna head uptown.

ONLY LOVE CAN BREAK YOUR HEART

Words and Music by
NEIL YOUNG

Only Love Can Break Your Heart - 2 - 1

Verse 2:
I have friends I've never seen,
He hides his head inside a dream.
Someone should call him and
See if he can come out,
Try to lose the down that he's found.
(To Chorus:)

THE ROAD

Words and Music by
DANNY O'KEEFE

Verses 1&2:

1. High - ways___ and dance___ halls;___ a good song takes you far.___
2. See additional lyrics

Rhy. Fig. 1

You write a - bout the moon,_____ and you

Verses 3&4:
w/Rhy. Fig. 1

3. Lad - ies come to see___ you if your name still rings a bell.__
4. *See additional lyrics*

They give you damn near noth - ing and they'll

say___ they knew_ you well.___ So you tell 'em you'll_ re - mem-

- ber, but they know it's just a game.___ And a - long the way_ their_

fac - es all___ be - gin_ to look_ the same.__

Chorus:
w/Rhy. Fig. 2

And when you stop to let 'em know_ you got it down,___ it's

Verse: 2
Coffee in the morning, cocaine afternoon
You talk about the weather and you grin about the ruin
Phone calls long distance, to tell you how you've been
You forget about the losses; you exagerate the wins.
(To Chorus:)

Verse 4:
Well, it isn't for the money, and it's only for a while
You stalk about the rooms and you roll away the miles
Gamblers in the neon clinging to guitars
You're right about the moon but you're wrong about the stars.
(To Chorus:)

TAKE IT EASY

Words and Music by
JACKSON BROWNE and GLENN FREY

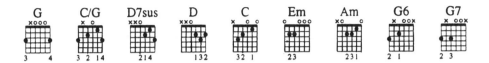

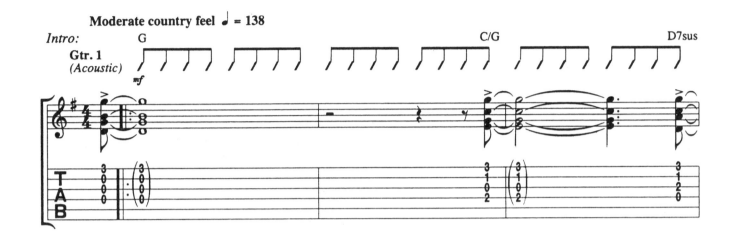

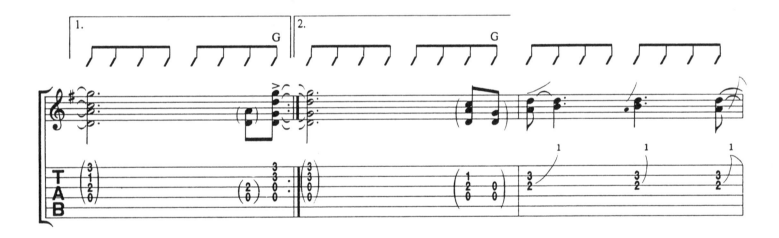

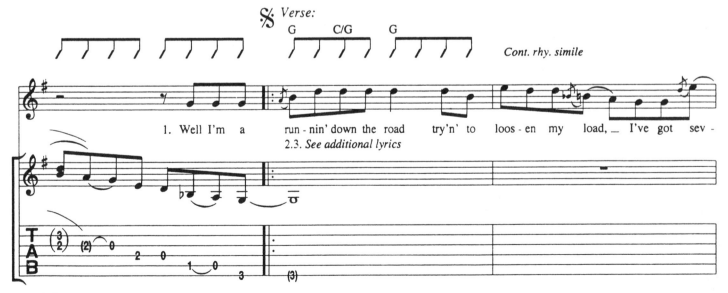

1. Well I'm a run-nin' down the road try'n' to loos-en my load, __ I've got sev-
2.3. *See additional lyrics*

Take It Easy - 4 - 1

*Substitute w/Am, Verse 3 only.

Chorus:

2. 3. *See additional lyrics*

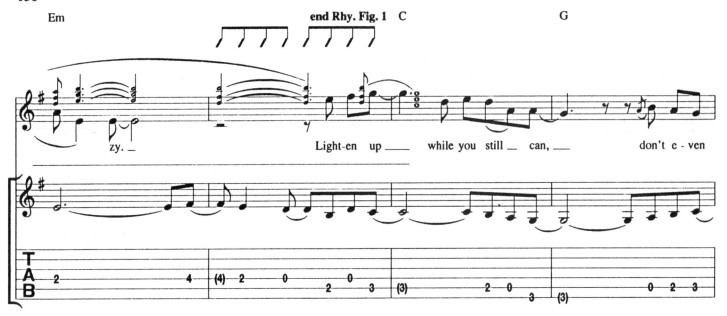

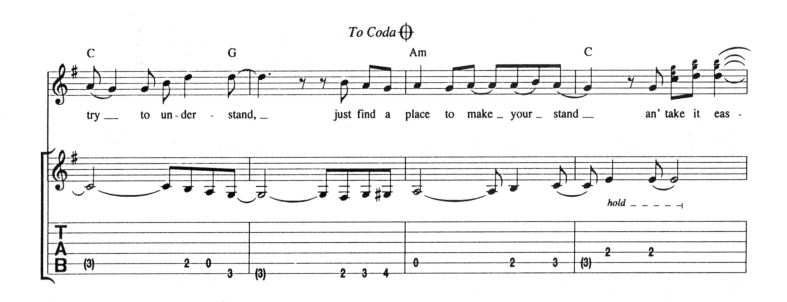

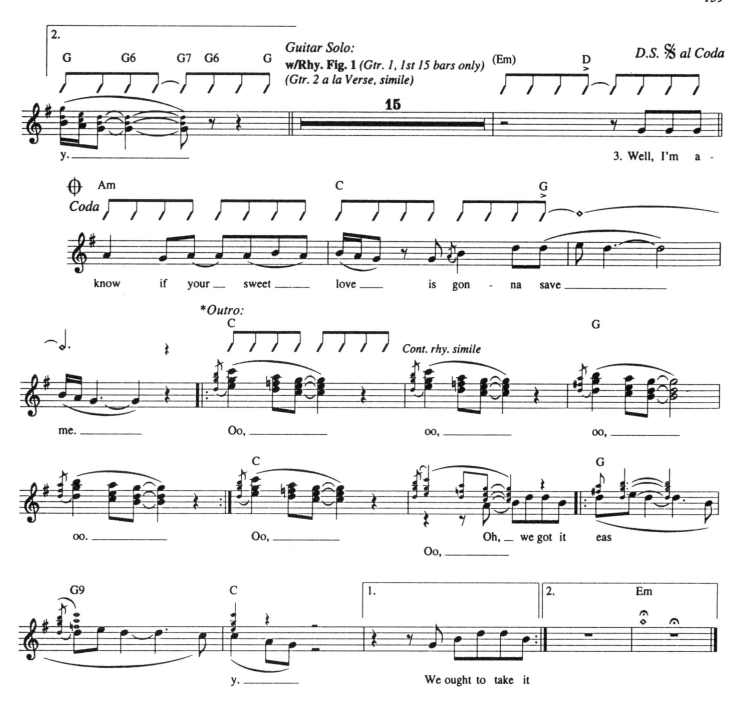

Verse 2:
Well, I'm a-standing on a corner in Winslow, Arizona,
And such a fine sight to see.
It's a girl, my lord, in a flatbed Ford
Slowing down to take a look at me.
(To Guitar Solo:)

Chorus 2:
Come on baby, don't say maybe.
I gotta know if your sweet love is gonna save me.
We may lose, and we may win.
Though we will never be here again.
So open up, I'm climbing in,
So take it easy.
(To Guitar Solo:)

Verse 3:
Well I'm a-running down the road,
Trying to loosen my load,
Gotta a world of trouble on my mind.
Looking for a lover who won't blow my cover,
She's so hard to find.
(To Chorus:)

Chorus 3:
Take it easy, take it easy.
Don't let the sound of your own wheels make you crazy.
Come on baby, don't say maybe.
I gotta know if your sweet love is gonna save me.
(To Coda)

ROSIE

**Words and Music by
JACKSON BROWNE and DONALD MILLER**

Rosie - 3 - 1

Ros - ie.___   Ros - ie.___

Ros - ie.___   Ros - ie.___

Verse 2:
Well, I sat her down right next to me,
And I got her a beer
While I mixed that sound on stage so the band could hear.
The more I watched her watch them play,
The less I thought of to say.
And when they walked off stage, the drummer
Swept that girl away.
(To Chorus:)

Verse 3:
Well, I guess I might have known from the start
She'd come for a star.
Could have told my imagination not to run too far.
Of all the times that I've been burned
By now you'd think I'd have learned
That it's who you look like, not who you are.
(To Chorus:)

SHOWER THE PEOPLE

Words and Music by
JAMES TAYLOR

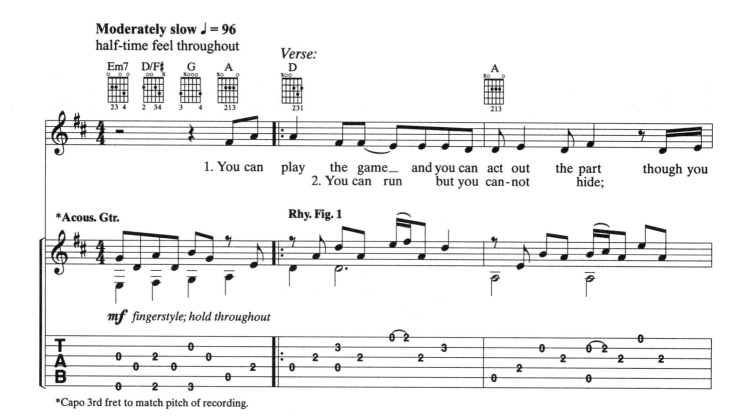

*Capo 3rd fret to match pitch of recording.

show them the way___ that you feel._____ Things are gon - na be much bet -

ter if you on - ly will.___

Acous. Gtr.

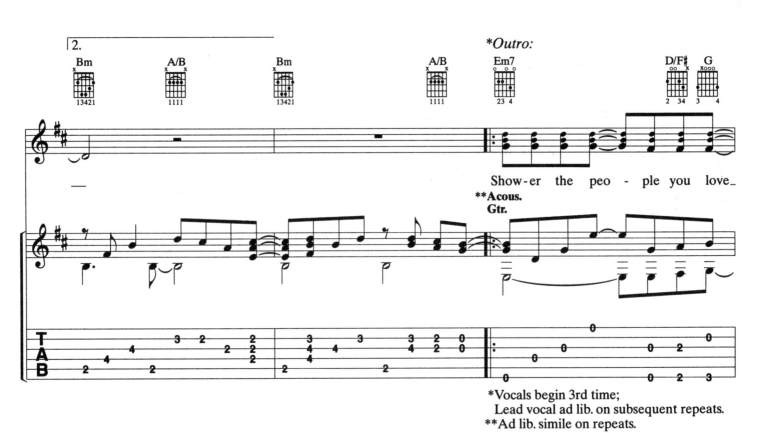

Show - er the peo - ple you love_

**Acous. Gtr.

*Vocals begin 3rd time;
Lead vocal ad lib. on subsequent repeats.
**Ad lib. simile on repeats.

Outro (vocal ad lib.):
They say in every life,
They say the rain must fall.
Just like a pouring rain,
Make it rain.
Love is sunshine.

SOCIETY'S CHILD
(a/k/a "Society's Child (Baby I've Been Thinking)")

Words and Music by
JANIS IAN

All gtrs. capo III

Moderately fast ♩ = 106

Intro:

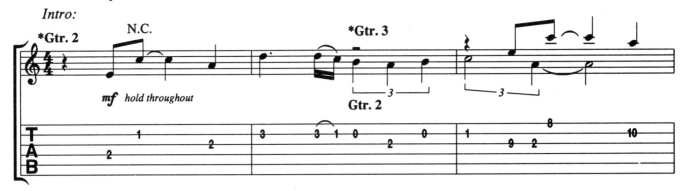

*Harpsichord arranged for two gtrs.

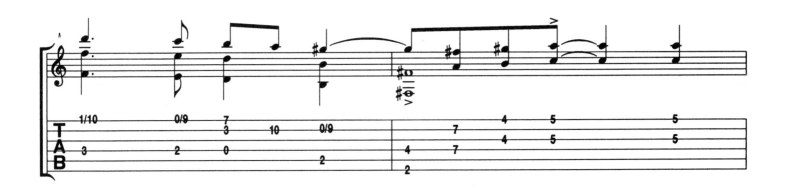

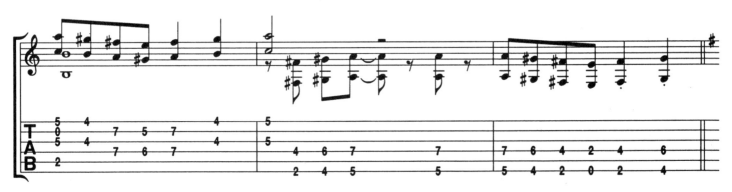

Society's Child – 3 – 1

Slower ♩ = 94

Chorus:

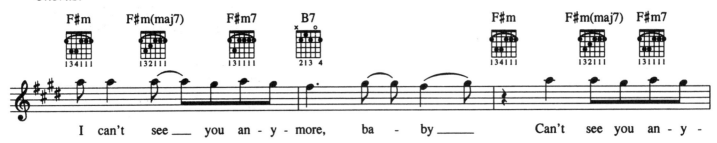

I can't see __ you an-y-more, ba — by ____ Can't see you an-y-

more. more. ____ No, I don't wan-na see you an-y-

more, ba — by. *rit. poco a poco*

Verse 2:
Walk me down to school, baby
Everybody's acting deaf and blind
Until they turn and say
"Why don't you stick to your own kind?"
My teachers all laugh, their smirking stares
Cutting deep down in our affairs
Preachers of equality
Think they believe it
Then why won't they just let us be?
(To Chorus:)

Verse 3:
One of these days I'm gonna stop my listening
Gonna raise my head up high
One of these days I'm gonna
Raise up my glistening wings and fly.
But that day will have to wait for a while,
Baby, I'm only society's child
When we're older, things may change
But for now this is the way they must remain.
(To Chorus:)

STRONG ENOUGH

Words and Music by
SHERYL CROW, KEVIN GILBERT, BRIAN MacLEOD,
DAVID RICKETTS, BILL BOTTRELL and DAVID BAERWALD

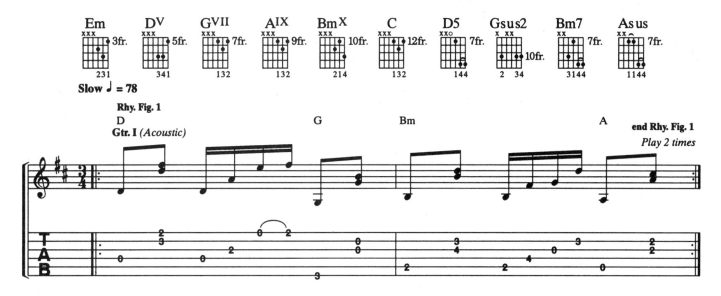

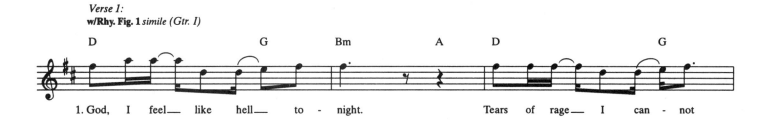

1. God, I feel___ like hell___ to - night. Tears of rage___ I can - not

fight   I'd be the last to help___ you un - der - stand. Are you

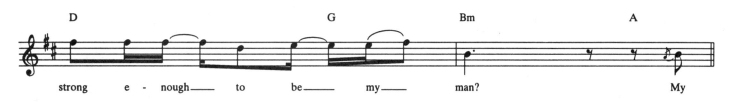

strong e - nough___ to be___ my___ man?   My

Strong Enough - 3 - 1

Verse 3:
I have a face I cannot show.
I make the rules up as I go.
It's try and love me if you can.
Are you strong enough to be my man?
My man.

Verse 4:
When I've shown you that I just don't care,
When I'm throwing punches in the air,
When I'm broken down and I can't stand,
Will you be man enough to be my man?

TAKE ME HOME, COUNTRY ROADS

Words and Music by
BILL DANOFF, TAFFY NIVERT
and JOHN DENVER

Take Me Home, Country Roads - 4 - 1

Take Me Home, Country Roads - 4 - 2

TAXI

Words and Music by
HARRY CHAPIN

Moderately ♩ = 60

Intro:

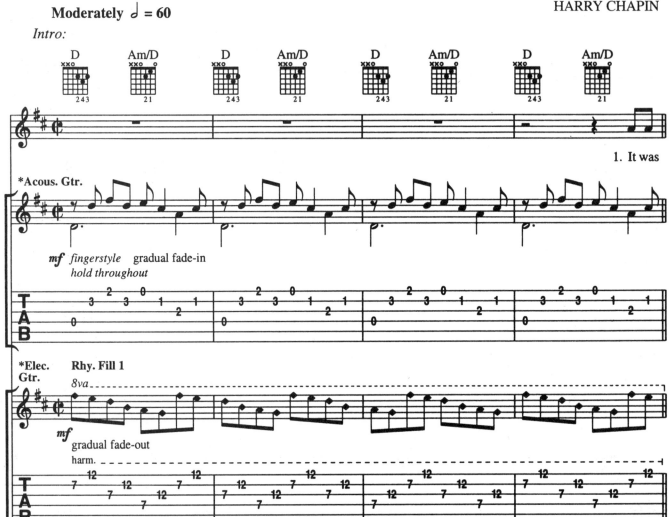

1. It was

*Acous. Gtr.

mf *fingerstyle* *gradual fade-in*
hold throughout

*Elec. Rhy. Fill 1
Gtr.*

mf *gradual fade-out*
harm.

*To match the studio recording, de-tune guitars down 1 whole step D, G, C, F, A, and D,
then place capo on 2nd fret after 2nd verse where indicated.

Verses 1, 3, & 8:

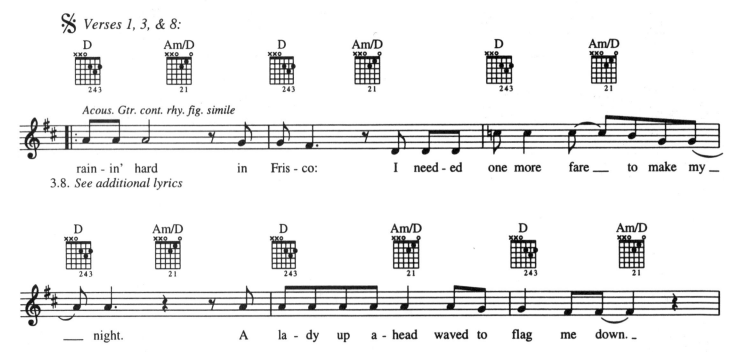

Acous. Gtr. cont. rhy. fig. simile

rain-in' hard   in Fris-co: I need-ed one more fare __ to make my __
3.8. *See additional lyrics*

__ night.   A la-dy up a-head waved to flag me down. _

Taxi - 8 - 1

*Capo 2nd fret for de-tuned guitar.

Verse 6:

w/Verse Rhy. Fig. *(Acous. Gtr.)* simile

some-where in a fair-y-tale; I used to take her home in my

car. We learned a-bout love in the back of a Dodge; __ the

w/Rhy. Fig. 1 *(Acous. Gtr.)* simile   Verse 7:
                                                        w/Rhy. Fig. 2 *(Acous. Gtr.)* simile

les-son had-n't gone too far. __   7. You see, she was gon-na be an

ac-tress, and I was gon-na learn to fly. __   She took off __ to find the

Taxi - 8 - 4

tide me o - ver 'til my time _____ runs _____

(falsetto) (O - ver _____ 'til my _____ time.)

Acous. Gtr. cont. rhy. fig. simile

_____ out. _____

Bridge 2:

Acous. Gtr. cont. rhy. fig. simile

*Ba - by's so high that she's sky - ing. _____

Acous. Gtr.

*Sung falsetto, 8va.

_____ Yes, she's fly - ing, _____ a-fraid to fall. _____ I'll tell you

why ba - by's cry - ing, _____ 'cause she's dy - ing, aren't we

D.S. 𝄋 al Coda

w/Rhy. Fill 1 (Elec. Gtr.) simile, gradual fade-out   w/Intro. Rhy. Fig. (Acous. Gtr.) simile

Acous. Gtr.

all? _____

8. There was

Taxi - 8 - 6

164

foot - lights. ___ I took off ___ for the sky. ___ 13. And here ___

Verse 13:

___ she's act - ing hap - py ___ in - side her hand - some home, ___ and

me, I'm fly - ing in my tax - i, tak - ing tips and get - ting ___ stoned.

Outro:

I go fly - ing so ___ high ___

___ when I'm ___ stoned. ___

Verse 3:
Something about her was familiar;
I could swear I'd seen her face before.
But she said, "I'm sure you're mistaken."
And she didn't say anything more.

Verse 4:
It took a while, but she looked in the mirror.
Then she glanced at the license for my name.
A smile seemed to come to her slowly;
It was a sad smile just the same.

Verse 8:
There was not much more for us to talk about;
Whatever we had once was gone.
So I turned my cab into the driveway,
Past the gate and the fine trimmed lawns.

Verse 9:
And she said, "We must get together,"
But I knew it'd never be arranged.
Then she handed me twenty dollars for a two-fifty fare;
She said, *(spoken)* "Harry, keep the change."

Taxi - 8 - 8

SUNSHINE ON MY SHOULDERS

Words and Music by
JOHN DENVER and MIKE TAYLOR

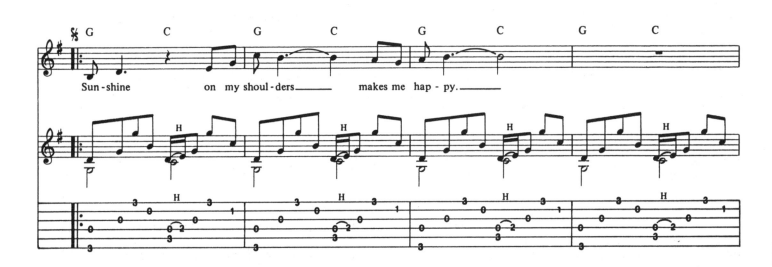

Sun-shine on my shoul-ders_____ makes me hap-py._____

Sun-shine in my eyes can make me cry._____

*To play along with recording, place capo at 3rd fret.

Sunshine on My Shoulders - 3 - 1

TIN MAN

Words and Music by
DEWEY BUNNELL

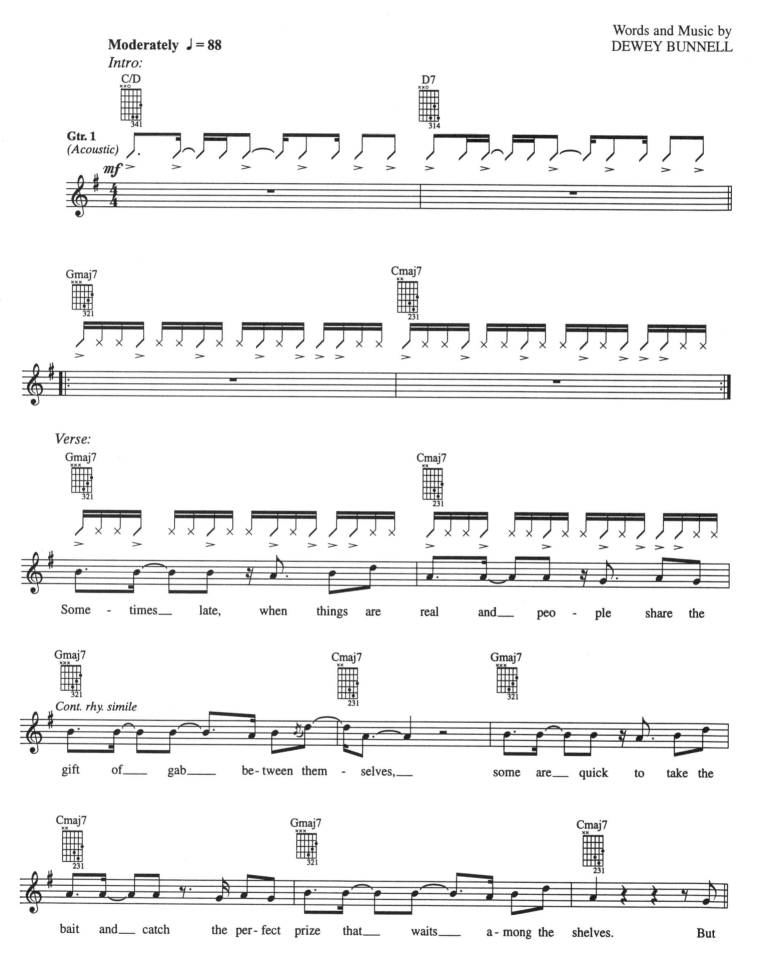

Tin Man - 3 - 1

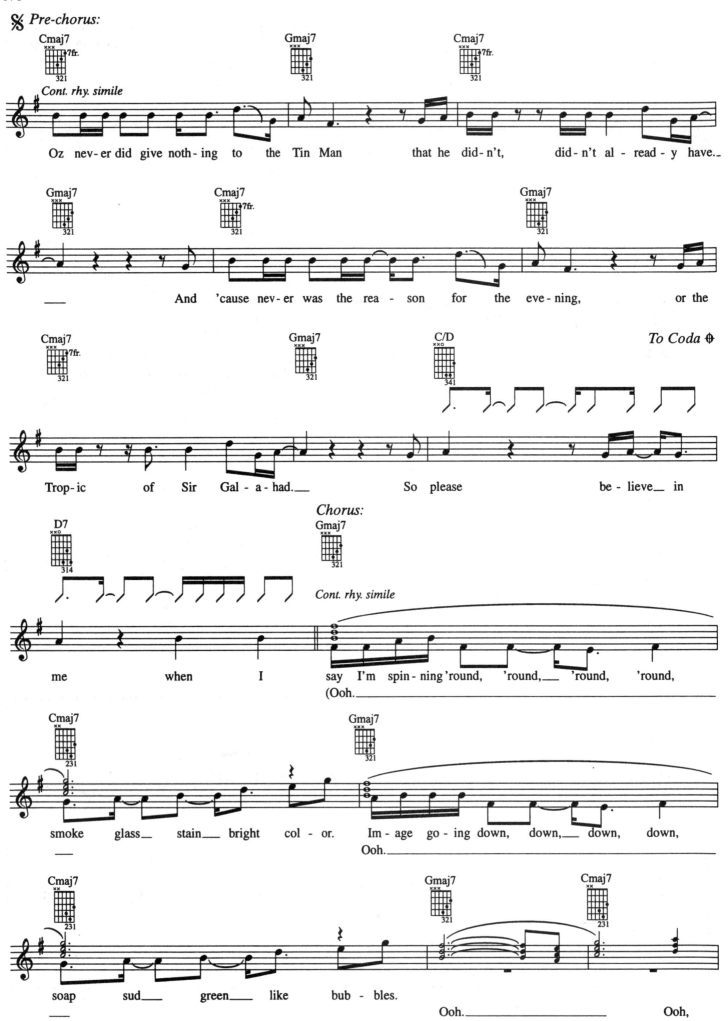

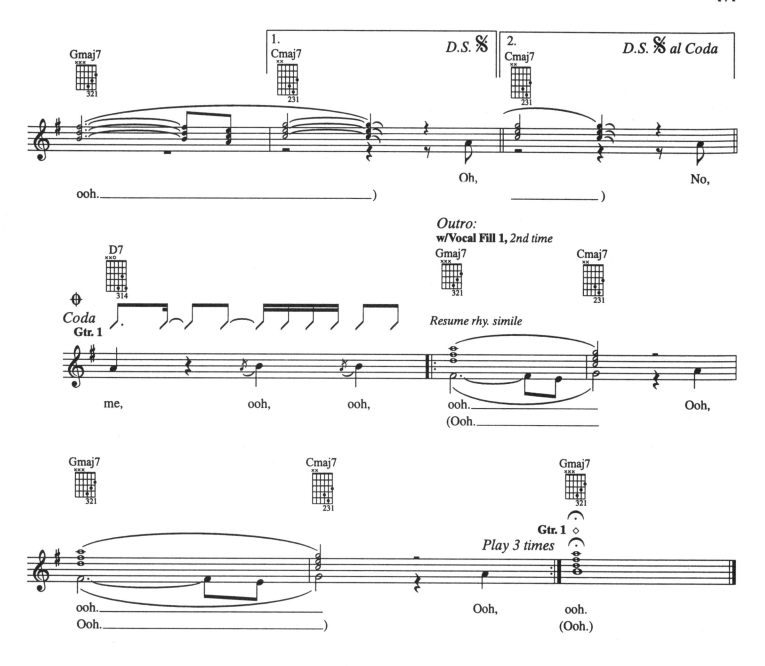

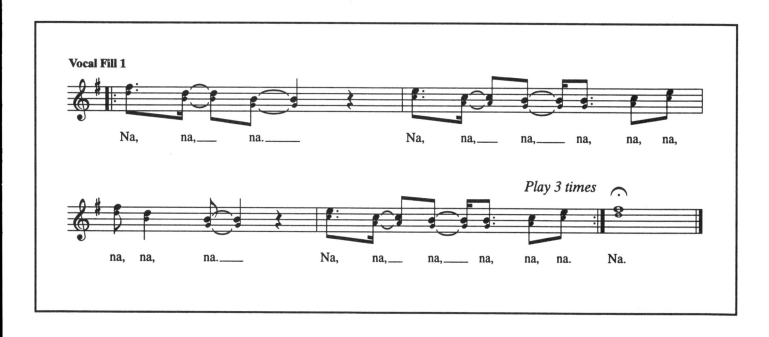

VINCENT
(Starry, Starry Night)

Words and Music by
DON McLEAN

Vincent (Starry, Starry Night) - 5 - 1

Vincent (Starry, Starry Night) - 5 - 2

Vincent (Starry, Starry Night) - 5 - 4

Vincent (Starry, Starry Night) - 5 - 5

WONDERING WHERE THE LIONS ARE

Acoustic Gtr. w/Drop D tuning: Capo II ⑥ = D

Moderately in 2 ♩ = 78

Intro:

Words and Music by
BRUCE COCKBURN

Thumb.

% *Verse:*

w/Rhy. Fig. 1 *(Acous. Gtr.)* 6 times, simile

1. Sun's up, mm, mm, looks o - kay.__ The world sur - vives__ in - to an - oth - er day__ and I'm
2. Walls, win - dows, trees, waves com - ing through,__ you be in me and I'll be in you to - geth -
3. 4. *See additional lyrics*

think - in' 'bout e - ter - ni - ty. Some__ kind of ec - sta - sy got a hold__
- er in e - ter - ni - ty. Some__ kind of ec - sta - sy got a hold__

To Coda ⊕

__ on me.__
__ on me.__ I

had an - oth - er dream a - bout li - ons at the door,__ they weren't half as fright - 'ning as they
Up a - mong the firs where it smells so sweet or down in the val - ley where the

Wondering Where the Lions Are - 3 - 1

178

Verse 3:
Huge orange flying boat rises off a lake.
Thousand year old petroglyphs doing a double take,
Pointing a finger at eternity.
I'm sitting in the middle of this ecstasy.
Young men marching, helmets shining in the sun,
Polished and precise like the brain behind the gun
(Should be!)
They got me thinking about eternity.
Some kind of ecstasy got a hold on me.
(To Chorus:)

Verse 4:
Freighters on the nod on the surface of the bay.
One of these days they're gonna sail away.
Gonna sail into eternity.
Some kind of ecstasy got a hold on me.
(To Outro Chorus:)

UNINVITED

Music and Lyrics by
ALANIS MORISSETTE

Slowly ♩ = 64

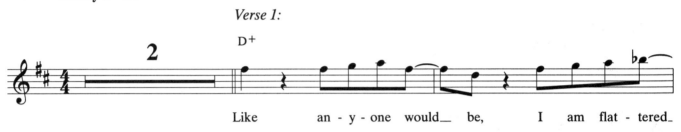

Verse 1:

Like an-y-one would__ be, I am flat-tered__

__ by your fas-ci-na-tion with__ me. Like an-y hot-blood-ed wom-

-an, I have sim-ply__ want-ed an ob-ject to crave.__ But

you, you're not__ al-lowed; you're un-in-vit-ed: an un-for-tu-

Verses 2 & 3:

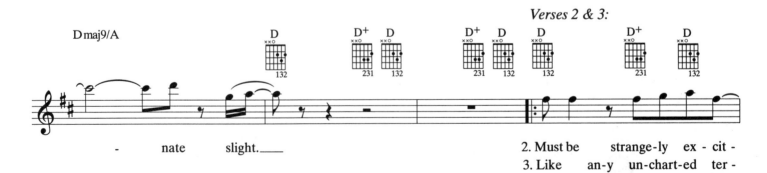

-nate slight.__

2. Must be strange-ly ex-cit-
3. Like an-y un-chart-ed ter-

WHO WILL SAVE YOUR SOUL

Words and Music by
JEWEL KILCHER

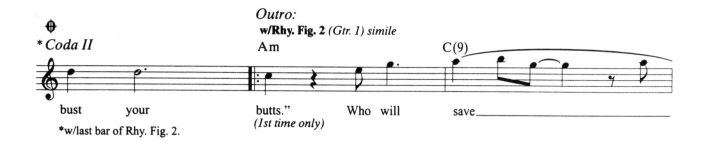

*Coda II

*w/last bar of Rhy. Fig. 2.

bust your butts." Who will save

Outro:
w/Rhy. Fig. 2 *(Gtr. 1) simile*

(1st time only)

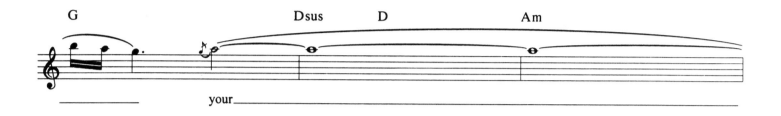

your

soul

*Repeat and fade

*Lead vocal ad lib on repeats.

Verse 3:
Some are walking, some are talking, some are stalking their kill.
Got social security, but that don't pay your bills.
There are addictions to feed and there are mouths to pay,
So you bargain with the devil, but you're O. K. for today.
Say that you love them, take their money and run.
Say, "It's been swell, sweetheart, but it was just one of those things,
Those flings, those strings you got to cut,
So get out on the streets, girls, and bust your butts."
(To Chorus:)

YOU WERE MEANT FOR ME

All gtrs. tune down 1/2 step:

⑥ = E♭   ③ = G♭

⑤ = A♭   ② = B♭

④ = D♭   ① = E♭

Words and Music by
JEWEL KILCHER and STEVE POLTZ

Moderately ♩ = 132

Intro:

Verse:

1. I hear the clock, it's six A. M., I feel so far from where I've been.
2.3. See additional lyrics

I got my eggs, I got my pan-cakes, too. I got my ma-ple syr-up, ev-'ry-thing but you.

w/Rhy. Fig. 1 (Gtr. 1)

I break the yokes and make a smile-y face,

You Were Meant for Me - 4 - 1

You Were Meant for Me - 4 - 2

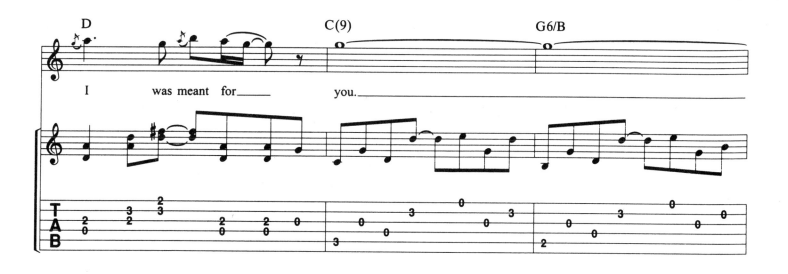

I was meant for_____ you._____

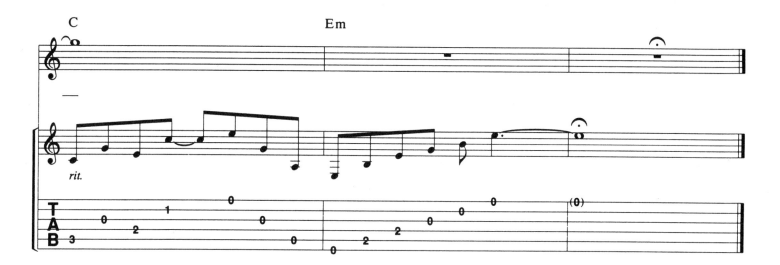

Verse 2:
I called my mama, she was out for a walk.
Consoled a cup of coffee, but it didn't wanna talk.
So I picked up a paper, it was more bad news.
More hearts being broken or people being used.
Put on my coat in the pouring rain.
I saw a movie, it just wasn't the same.
'Cause it was happy and I was sad
And it made me miss you, oh, so bad.
(To Chorus:)

Verse 3:
I brush my teeth and put the cap back on.
I know you hate it when I leave the light on.
I pick a book up and then I turn the sheets down,
And then I take a deep breath and a good look around.
Put on my pj's and hop into bed.
I'm half alive, but I feel mostly dead.
I try and tell myself it'll be all right,
I just shouldn't think anymore tonight.
(To Chorus:)

YOU LEARN

Lyrics by
ALANIS MORISSETTE
Music by
ALANIS MORISSETTE and GLEN BALLARD

You Learn - 3 - 1

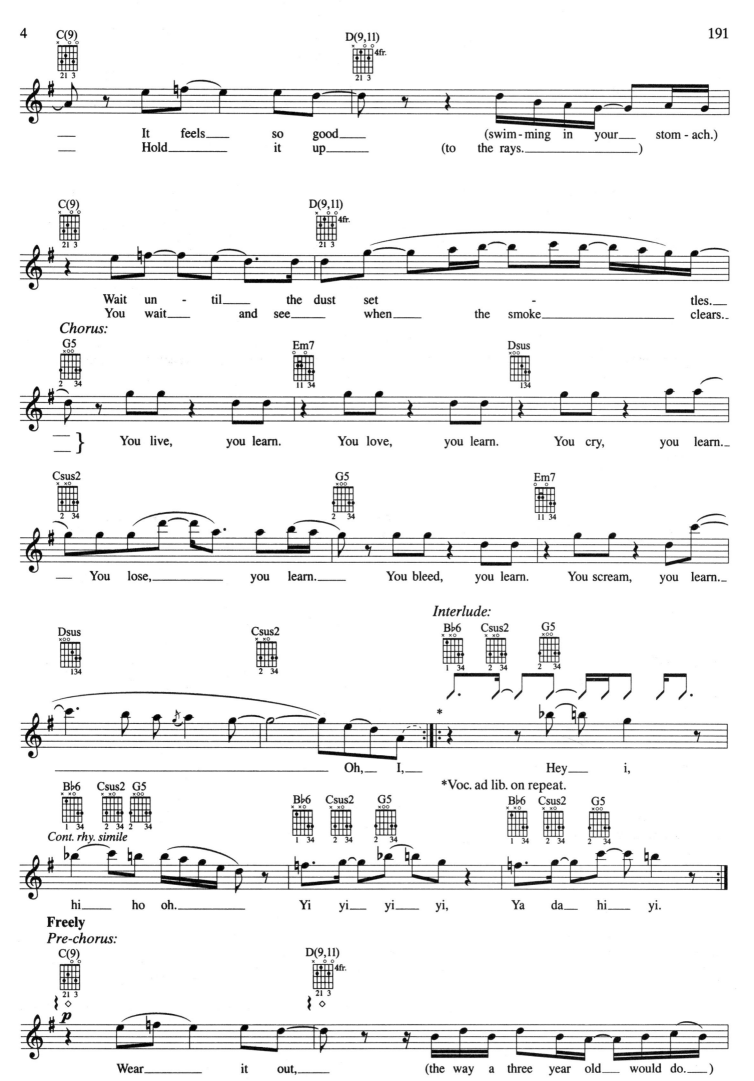

It feels___ so good___ (swim-ming in your___ stom - ach.)
Hold_____ it up___ (to the rays._____)

Wait un - til___ the dust set - - - tles.___
You wait___ and see___ when___ the smoke_____ clears..

Chorus:

___ } You live, you learn. You love, you learn. You cry, you learn._

___ You lose,___ you learn.___ You bleed, you learn. You scream, you learn._

Interlude:

Oh,__ I,__ Hey__ i,

*Voc. ad lib. on repeat.

Cont. rhy. simile

hi___ ho oh._____ Yi yi__ yi___ yi, Ya da__ hi__ yi.

Freely
Pre-chorus:

Wear_____ it out,___ (the way a three year old___ would do.___)

192

Melt_____ it down,___ you're gon - na have to e - ven - tu - 'lly an - y - way.

In time

cresc.

The fi - re trucks___ are com - ing up a - round the bend.___

Chorus:

_____ 1. You live, you learn. You love, you learn. You cry, you learn.___

2. You grieve, you learn. You choke, you learn. You laugh, you learn.___

1.

— You lose,_____ you learn._____ You bleed, you learn. You scream, you learn.___

— You choose,_____ you learn._____ You pray, you learn.

2.

You ask, you learn.

Free time

You live, you learn._____